PRAISE FOR A PL

“In Janet Ross’s memoir, yo … venture, decades of environmental history, insights into place-based educational philosophy, and warm portraits of a lifetime of encounters with the people of the West. But her goal here is personal—celebrating the panels in her life’s quilt, a life richly rooted in the redrock canyons of the Colorado Plateau.

Her quilting mentor taught her, ‘perspective is everything.’ In this book, Ross does her mentor proud. By ‘pressing the seams of this place into her life,’ she found the perspective she has been seeking for a lifetime.”

Stephen Trimble, editor of *Red Rock Stories: Three Generations of Writers Speak on Behalf of Utah’s Public Lands* and *The Capitol Reef Reader*

“Janet Ross has a crucial story to tell about what it means to create not only a sense of place in the rural Southwest, but embody and foster an ethic of place. Through the metaphor of quilting, she shows how one creates a meaningful life by piecing together what appear to be disparate fabrics into a cohesive whole. Janet Ross’s story belongs to the tradition of western women from Mary Austin to Maureen Whipple to Ellen Meloy. What this woman knows about independence and interdependence in the name of community and social change, we need to hear.”

Terry Tempest Williams, author of *Refuge: An Unnatural History of Family and Place*

“A Place Called Home *is a warm, cuddly quilt to wrap yourself inside of. It’s also a rip-roaring account of remarkable life experiences. Hard to believe that one woman has managed to pack this many adventures into one life. From deep in the city to deep in the wilderness, Janet has woven all these experiences into a life of commitment to home on the Colorado Plateau and to the important role sense of place plays in finding happiness."*

David Sobel, Professor Emeritus, Education Department, Antioch University New England and author of *Place-Based Education: Connecting Classrooms and Communities*

"If our lives are patchwork quilts, how many panels represent home? Janet Ross spent her life seeking and finding her home place, loving and listening to the Colorado Plateau, creating outdoor experiences that taught countless diverse students how to appreciate, understand, and love the land. It's a life well lived, and Janet has sewn together a place-based memoir well worth reading."

Toby McLeod, Director, Sacred Land Film Project

"I loved reading about Emma's Happiness Museum and Janet's descriptions made it come alive, as well as her pleasure in knowing an exceptional woman. The sustained metaphor of quilting really works; since I quilt it really spoke to me, and on other levels as well – growing up, family, her view of the world. This is a quality piece of work of which the author can be proud."

Ann Zwinger (in memoriam), author of *Wind in the Rock: The Canyonlands of Southeastern Utah*

"As a metaphor and organizing principle, the quilt works well...Janet carries it throughout in a way that makes sense and holds the book together."

Ellen Meloy (in memoriam), author of *The Anthropology of Turquoise: Reflections on Desert, Sea, Stone, and Sky*

A Place Called Home

Quilting a Life of Joy on the Colorado Plateau

Janet Ross

Foreword by Craig Childs

Cover and interior illustrations by Kai Standy

Lost Souls press

Published in the United States by
Lost Souls Press
Colorado
www.lostsoulspress.com

ISBN 978-1-7346553-5-3

Dedication

To the Colorado Plateau*—Where I found the idea fabric for my place-based life*

To my parents*—I enjoyed every stitch of time on this earth with you*

To Emma*—My life quilt inspiration*

Contents

PART THREE

Place as the Binding of a Life Quilt

PART FOUR

Using the Six P's to Prepare the Life Quilt Sandwich

PART FIVE

Adaptability to Inevitable Change Quilts a Life Together

Foreword

I used to live in a tepee back in the days before indoor plumbing or electricity. In the tepee, mice ate holes in my clothes, even if I dropped them on the floor for just overnight. They chewed out my hems and elbows. I live in a cabin now, and mice are still eating holes in my clothes. That has left me with a good deal of fabric. I still cut out pockets and save belt loops. Buttons are sewn onto other garments with off-colored thread to remind me of what was cut, what was saved, what was lost. I wear whole wardrobes sometimes in one sitting, in one pair of pants, one shirt, or one pack on my shoulders.

Aren't we all this way, stitched together from whatever we could find, from half-ruined junk and priceless bolts of fabric so carefully chosen? That is where this book leads me, then out the door and past the road into the wilderness.

Some of us are thrown onto the landscape drifting

from place to place, registering the length of the Grand Canyon and the sickly smell of truck brakes burning on Highway 191 through Bluff. We sew each piece of the earth together with our memories, creating a landscape out of our minds. And one day we realize we are no longer drifting but are pacing back and forth across a couple of million square miles of ground. The Center of the Universe, some Hopi have called it, the *axis mundi* say others. We keep on our shelves memories of this place. We pick them up every now and then, stones and feathers we have gathered over the years, old books of maps, letters from good friends in nearby towns. We hold these in our hands and remember the various horizons rooted into us, as if standing in many places at once, stretched almost palpably across the land.

Now sitting at my desk down a path cleared between stacks of papers and books. Maps hang off every wall and even off the ceiling. Maybe a hundred photographs of places and artifacts are tacked across one another like a madman's wallpaper. I am surrounded by the Southwest, black and white satellite images of Chinle Wash posted ceiling to floor, skulls of foxes and wildcats strung over the windowsill, and a grit all over the floorboards, pale sand from the Gran Desierto hauled back in pockets and sleeves.

And before me is this manuscript, a record of places and moments I know all so well, ringing in my ears like thunder across sandstone.

CRAIG CHILDS
West Elk Mountain
Spring 2006

Preface

"Quilts are irresistible. The lure of traditional patterns and the sense of continuity they evoke, together with the excitement of contemporary design and the potential for new art, all contribute." [1]

A Place Called Home: Quilting a Life of Joy on the Colorado Plateau is a place-based creative non-fiction memoir at its heart. It is a collection of stories about how finding my "place" was essential to finding my happiness. It is a template for others to find their own happiness within natural and human communities, inspired by a love of a place that calls them home.

A Place Called Home was inspired by an early mentor, quiltmaker, and operator of a Happiness Museum, Emma Andres. Thus I use the stages of quiltmaking as a metaphor, with my life quilt blocks of love, family, work, spirituality, humor, sense of place, prior planning, and adaptability to inevitable change, pieced together with the science of happiness.

I stitched my life around the 130,000 square-mile Colorado Plateau. After discovering a strong sense of place early in life, and later developing a commitment to educating others about its value and protection, I founded the place-based Four Corners School of Outdoor Education (FCS) in 1984. With determination and perseverance in my rural, sometimes hostile, often inspiring Monticello, Utah my life's work culminated with the building of a new campus for FCS, the Canyon Country Discovery Center, from which I retired at the end of 2016. It is from a life filled with purpose and a sense of place that I found happiness.

Emma Andres, an early inspiration to me as a Prescott College student (1971-1974), was an accomplished quilter in Prescott, Arizona (1902-1987). She operated Emma's Happiness Museum (1963-1984), and was a featured quilter in *Grand Endeavors: Vintage Arizona Quilts and Their Makers* (Northland Press, 1992). Her life story and artistry inspired me early on to craft a meaningful life, as I too am a quilter and quilt collector. Her love of home, place, family and quilting were where she found happiness.

Happiness is a universal desire and, according to the U.S. Declaration of Independence, an inalienable right of Americans to pursue. How to find and keep happiness is something that has been written about by hundreds of authors and researchers, such as how we: are hard-wired for happiness; control our own happiness; choose happiness; enhance it by having a positive attitude toward life; and discover it by chance from our genetics, beliefs, magic, or good karma. The importance of "sense of place" in finding and sustaining happiness has not been part of that conversation. I believe a sense of place is essential to our finding happiness, from a blend of pure biology and cosmic serendipity, some of which we can simply recognize, and some we can manage, if not control.

I believe that from a sense of place we form a commitment to protect the place where we feel most at home. In a dictionary sense, anywhere can be a "place." But some places just speak to you, fill your heart with joy, even cause physical changes at a cellular level—they are that important to your happiness. That could be anywhere really—the outdoors in general; a specific landscape; a city; your house; with your soulmate; in a church; on a stage singing your truth; or where generations of your family have lived. It's any place YOU feel most at home and choose to be. For me it was first the outdoor world in all its forms, and later the landscapes of the Colorado Plateau, which I worked to educate about and protect for many years.

Of course, globally there is much inequality in an individual's ability to find and keep happiness. If you only look at economic and political factors such as wealth, social freedom, good health care, social safety net, meaningful work, lack of corruption, social trust and compassion, and public policy, it would be impossible for 80 percent of the people of the world to find happiness. And of course, sometimes a strong sense of place can also lead to anger, hate, violence, and even war, from a commitment to hold onto that place by demonizing the "other."

I believe that if one finds a place that invokes a strong sense of love, and is also mixed with a sense of cultural identity, the fear of losing or sharing that place can be overcome. If one can find a place to call home, and thus find personal happiness, it can lead to positive loving, social and environmental outcomes. Otherwise, happiness would be, as economist and social scientist Eduard Punset wrote, just "*an emotional state activated by the limbic system in which the conscious brain has as little to say as it has in what happens with the billions of membranes that protect their respective nuclei and make our organism a walking community of cells."* [2]

This book, in stitching the many blocks of my place-based life quilt together, is a tribute to my mother who was a consummate storyteller, reading teacher, and lover of happy tales; and to my father, one of the happiest people I knew for all of his 98+ years. It is also a love letter to the Colorado Plateau, that has called me home, and I have called home for over 45 years.

....

"It is neither wealth nor splendor, but tranquility and occupation which gives happiness."

- Thomas Jefferson

....

Part One

LOVE, FAMILY, WORK, AND SPIRITUALITY AS THE IDEA FABRIC FOR A LIFE QUILT

"A quilt is a bedcover made of two pieces of cloth with some kind of filler between. The American quilt is a combination of several needle arts, all of which have histories that predate the written word." [3]

Chapter 1

Color Recipe

"Without light there is no color. Use, enjoy, have, embrace color, because when you are dead there is no color ... Open your mind to color ... Color is light." [4]

IN THE FALL OF 1967 WHEN I FIRST READ ABOUT PRESCOTT College in Prescott, Arizona in *Time* magazine, I wondered if I had found my colorful life calling. It was on the southern end of a place I had heard of, but had never been: the Colorado Plateau. The college was designed to train outdoor leaders, environmental educators, and used an outdoor classroom. I eagerly applied to enter after my junior year of high school.

When my mother and I flew from St. Louis, Missouri to visit its campus, I found myself involuntarily take a long, deep breath while looking up at the vast blue sky, and saluting the giant sage-green saguaro cactus standing tall on the beige indoor-outdoor carpeted desert floor, as we drove north from Phoenix toward Prescott. The cholla prickly sticks and wobbly octopus-like ocotillo cactus arms waved back as we passed by them. The pale green Sonoran desert slowly melted into sage green scrub oak, then into dark green piñon and juniper forest as we gained elevation on the interstate. On the far horizon were the snowcapped green-brown San Francisco Peaks near Flagstaff. I drew a heart-shaped patch of sage and dark greens in my journal. After we arrived at the college, with its red-pink Granite Mountain backdrop, I toured the campus, interviewed, then waited two months for a response. The news was bad: I was not accepted. I applied again to start after my senior year and again was rejected.

I was accepted to Oregon State University, so reluctantly began college at this agriculture, forestry, and research school, as far from my parents and the Midwest as I could get. I explored this wet, dark-green, densely forested world, hiking in lava tube caves, soaking in hot springs, and protesting at OSU basketball games against Brigham Young University's prohibition on black men joining the Mormon priesthood since they were not "white and delightsome," a teaching of the church until 1981. During the first semester, I signed up for a class on "Wilderness"—its history, philosophy, politics, and management practices, six years after Congress passed the Wilderness Act. I was enchanted by the idea of a place where man was a visitor and could not remain. I actually knew little of true Wilderness (with a capital 'W'). In the 'lowercase wilderness' I had trekked as a Girl Scout in the Missouri Ozarks, where human activity like roads and farms were often visible. So, I wondered what the big "W" would be like, an area essentially undisturbed by human activity, with a naturally developed community of life.

I was also enchanted by my class teacher, who taught Wilderness politics *and* worked as a forester. He furthered my developing interest in bluegrass music, whose proud lead instrument was the banjo, the extrovert of musical instruments—always fun, sometimes rowdy, a comedian of sorts—and taught me a Buck Owens song "Three Dimension Love,"—*"My love is deeper than the ocean, higher than the sky..."* We listened to "Dueling Banjos" from the movie *Deliverance*, about four men who canoe down a river in the remote northern Georgia Wilderness, expecting to have fun, and witness unspoiled nature before the fictional Cahulawassee River valley was flooded by construction of a dam. The song foretold darkness that occurred along the way. But the banjo made me dance and clap with its bright, twangy, rippling, joyful tone, unlike my usual introverted self. And my cerebral mass began to see other bright and codified signals in the universe. I did not see any darkness at this point in my life.

My college Wilderness class teacher, now my boyfriend, invited me to hitchhike through Alaska with him that summer to show me the big "W" up close—on my first grand adventure! I took the Alaska Marine Highway ferry from Seattle to Wrangell to join him and we made several more stops before Haines where we started hitchhiking. Along the way we baked bread over a campfire, watched the red-blue-purple-green northern lights, slept under a blanket of black sky full of stars, before eventually falling asleep in the Yukon Territories of Canada. We passed through incredible landscapes of dark green, dense, and humid forests and eventually watched brown grizzly bears run through the tundra near Denali National Park. But something in me yearned more for the open, expansive, dry landscape I had visited two years before in Arizona. I longed to be rid of humidity, mold, and wet clothes, and dreamed of awakening each morning to long distance views of red rocks and blue sky, cactus, green-gray sagebrush and juniper trees, followed by an even blacker night full of a billion yellow stars.

My forester friend saw the world as managed ecosystems within increasingly complex social environments. At 19, I wasn't ready to be managed as part of a complex social system. I applied again in spring 1971 to Prescott College and was finally accepted. I left him and Alaska at summer's end for an arid green educational adventure in Arizona, the place I wanted to be. We sang our last song together, "The Frozen Logger" by James Stevens, *"And so I lost my lover and to this cafe I come, to search each day for someone who stirs his coffee with his thumb..."*

Some scientists think color is actually not something you really see, but an interference pattern between the universe and our visual perception—a route followed by codified signals from a photon to the retina to specific neurons in the brain. Others say that certain colors connect us with certain moods, emotions, or values we associate with positive experiences, and that color preference is strongly influenced by culture. I hoped this next grand adventure would be very colorful!

THIS BLOCK OF MY LIFE QUILT IS A BANJO AND A BIG "W."

Chapter 2

Creating a Life Quilt

....

"Quilts [were] made in every territory and state, as a vital expression of the hopes, desires, frustrations, and sorrows of American women over the last 200 years." [5]

....

Quilts have been fashioned out of everything from rough homespun cloth to elegant silk as an expression of women's lives.

DURING ONE OF MY MANY WEEKLY WANDERINGS THROUGH THE downtown streets of Prescott, Arizona in fall of 1971, I saw a narrow door with a small sign that said "cigars," squeezed between a hardware store and J.C. Penney's. I stopped immediately, and looked up at a larger wooden sign with hand-painted letters in large, shaky, black loops that said: *Emma's Happiness Museum*. I tried the door, but it was locked. Inside I saw many intriguing looking quilts, made of all types of cloth. But it was closed, so I went back to my Prescott College classes—Rock Climbing 101 in the Granite Dells, whitewater kayaking on the Colorado River, sea kayaking along the Baja coast, and backpacking Copper Canyon in Mexico.

In February, between skiing in Yellowstone and climbing the volcanoes in Mexico, I went downtown to check the museum's door once again. My luck had changed; the lights were on, and the door open. I peered into what seemed a small space, but maybe that was because it was packed with displays. I could see two rooms and smelled musty cigars. There was barely enough space to walk between the glass cases, but I sidled down a passageway toward the back. An older woman approached me before I was two feet down the passageway. She was five foot two, late 60s, wore a bright red dress, and had matching circles of rouge on her cheeks. Her mop of dark curly hair was crowned with big red roses on a red straw hat. Other guests milled inside, but she beelined right for me. She smiled and shouted, "Hello, come right in, I'll take you on a tour! I'm Emma Mary Martha Andres—the first letter of each part of my full name spells

Emma, so that's what folks call me. Where are you from, and why are you in Prescott?" Before I could answer, she placed her hand on the small of my back, and with a wave of the other pointed while walking me toward a quilt hanging on the wall.

Without a pause, she told me that folks described her museum as "just like the Grand Canyon! Every time you look, you see something different." The flowers on her hat punctuated her laughter, bobbing with each chuckle. She peppered me with information, never giving me time to ask a question, as she led me around the museum, pulling things out of cases, explaining them and putting them back. She showed me a newspaper clipping about an award she had won at a quilt show, then a ceramic doll that was hand-painted, wearing a red dress and black hat, made by Carrie Hall, a nationally renowned doll maker from North Platte, Nebraska. She held up a picture of an elderly man in a rocking chair with a quilt in his lap, a needle between his fingers, and told me he was Charles (Dad) Pratt, one of the few male quilters in the U.S. and exceptional at the craft. She pointed to her copy of his Good Shepherd quilt hanging on the wall with Jesus standing straight and tall with his staff, one sheep draped over his shoulders, another standing by his side. Pointing to another quilt called Woman Spinning, she said it won a green ribbon at the Los Angeles regional round of the Sears Quilt Contest at the 1933 Chicago World's Fair.

I barely remembered what I had learned in class the day before, but was learning new things every second as she shared her memories. She showed me her many scrapbooks, where she had written all the names, dates and places of her awards, correspondence, and ideas, in case she forgot. Maybe I should start a journal, I thought. Reading old memories might be important in my future, like remembering what Emma looked like. Smells too might create important future memories if I wrote them down, like the cigar smells of the museum, because of the tiny chemical substances that attached themselves to receptors on my sensory cells, went to the olfactory area of my brain, and ultimately created an emotional response and a memory. Sounds as well might create future memories, of quilting stories and Emma, after being passed to my brain by the movements of hair cells called cilia, which produced a series of brief electrical signals from a sudden burst of acoustic information.

That day I started creating file folders of journal entries in which to place memories of smells, sights, and sounds, to reexamine later. I started with my childhood: the smell of musty mildew log cabins, stinky ginkgo pods, wet green clover-scented grass, the sweet smell of honeysuckle nectar, wet dusty sand in my nose rolling down a sand dune, and the salty seaweed fishy ocean.

Plus the sound of a whippoorwill's repeated call, loud crickets chirping, loons whistling, bobwhite-bobwhite-bobwhite, the sounds of my father and mother singing "Found a Peanut," "The Worms Crawl In, the Worms Crawl Out," and "The Ants Go Marching One by One."

The sounds of paddling a canoe for hour after hour—dip after dip—with a loon's long minor key song repeated over and over filled my file folders. As did walking or running home in the rain through puddles of cold rainwater, sitting on the roof naked in a torrential rainstorm, hearing rumbles overhead, a distant tornado swirling by, my head throbbing from the high barometric pressure, with clouds boiling in the dark sky.

Nearly two hours later, I was still there, listening to Emma's stories. Yet as she spoke, my eyes kept darting back to one specific quilt on the wall. She noticed and asked, "So you want to know more about that quilt, do you?" I nodded eagerly as she led me to the one she called the Desert Appliqué, the first quilt that had caught my eye through the door months earlier. It was made up of 14 blocks with a bright yellow background. Each block contained several green cacti—saguaro, yucca, prickly pear, and ocotillo—along with a purple mountain and small rattlesnake, all under a blue sky with puffy, lazy white clouds. Now that I was closer I could read the words stitched in the center: “Out Where the West Begins,” by Arthur Chapman:

> Out where the handclasp’s a little stronger
> Out where the smile dwells a little longer
> That’s where the west begins.
> Out where the sun is a little brighter,
> Where the snows that fall are a trifle whiter,
> Where the bonds of home are a wee bit tighter
> That’s where the west begins.

Emma kept right on talking, while I re-read the poem, memorizing every word. Suddenly, she said, “The whole thing in here is an education. It’s been like a college to me. I never went anywhere, but I’ve met people from all over.”

My head snapped back. “The Prescott College motto, where I attend school is, ‘Education is a journey, not a destination,’” I said, and laughed. “Will you teach me to make a quilt and how to collect good quality quilts?”

Her face turned as red as her rouge and her eyes welled up as she exclaimed, “Why, of course!”

She signed my independent study form a week later, and we agreed to meet weekly on Tuesdays. This gave me an excuse to visit Emma more often at the museum and her house. For the next three months, Emma helped me create many different sample quilt blocks: a wedding ring, a flying goose, a lone star, a heart basket, and an embroidered picture of a horse. It seemed my sampler quilt blocks—with a variety of fabrics, patterns, colors, and themes—began to unite into a series of harmonious design vignettes of my interests. As we stitched, I shared other college class experiences with her as windows into my life—the Colorado Plateau life zones, learning to kayak at Lees Ferry on the Colorado River, and the acronym for the layers of rock in the Grand Canyon I had learned while backpacking: Know The Canyon's History Study Rocks Made By Time (Kaibab, Toroweap, Coconino, Hermit, Supai, Redwall, Muav, Bright Angel, Tapeats). After leading a freshman orientation group backpacking through the Wilderness of the Plateau life zones for a month, starting in the brown-gray Douglas Fir and aspen **Canadian Zone** of the Aquarius Plateau, descending into the green-brown ponderosa pine, piñon and juniper **Transition and upper Sonoran life zones** of Capitol Reef, then descending into more of the gray-green upper **Sonoran zone** of the Burr Desert, climbing back up into the light-dark green **Hudsonian zone** of fir and spruce trees, to the gray-brown **Arctic-alpine zone** of lichens and moss of the orange-gray granite laccolithic Henry Mountains, I told her I felt these places and activities were setting a stage for the rest of my life, a happiness museum of sorts, like a collection of artifacts, experiences, and objects of artistic, cultural, historical, and scientific importance to me.

Emma responded, "I use my museum windows as a little stage of their own, and they are always deeply inspired. My windows don't amount to a 'dern,' but they've got a lot of love in them. I try to keep them simple and childlike."

Every time I was in town that fall and winter, I went by Emma's Happiness Museum to read its ever-changing window messages, always heartfelt. In December, the museum's window featured seven wooden reindeer, a plastic Santa Claus, fake snow, a Jesus picture, paper hearts and a three-by-five-inch card that said, "The Good Shepherd is my lifeline." In a corner were several black and brown rocks, colorful plastic flowers sticking out of a pile of sand, and a three-by-five card that read, "The earth is my Shepherd." Each object must have a story behind it, connected in some way to why I was drawn here, or, as Emma said later, connected by miracles. But I had yet to ask Emma herself whether her museum helped people find happiness, or just expressed what made her happy. I continued to drop by the museum often and, if it was open, stare at the many quilts: the Desert Appliqué, and another made of red and white fabric with the flowers of all 50 states embroidered on it, and the state's name stitched above each flower. Utah was the sego lily, Colorado the columbine, Alaska fireweed, and Wyoming Indian paintbrush. I had learned some local flower names in my first semester at Prescott College, so was learning more in this museum. I also saw display cases full of thimbles, buttons, and ceramic dolls. There were newspaper clippings, what looked like journals, vases of plastic flowers, photographs on top of glass cases, and small paintings on the walls. There must be a story for all of them.

Somehow I knew her Happiness Museum, Prescott College, and the Colorado Plateau life zones would become vitally important in my life. Over the next eight years I visited other deserts—Mojave, Great Basin, and Chihuahuan. I revisited the wet landscapes of my midwestern youth and Alaska. But no landscape pulled me back the way the Colorado Plateau did. This was where my heart-brain felt at home.

THIS BLOCK OF MY QUILT WILL BE EMMA'S HEAD AND FACE FRAMED BY A LARGE RED HAT WITH A CLUSTER OF RED ROSES SPILLING OVER THE BRIM. HIDING BEHIND THE FLOWERS ARE HER LAUGHING, TWINKLING EYES.

Chapter 3

Design Principles

"[Making] quilts wasn't something I ever planned to do ... I found the quilt (designs) I tended to like were ones which showed great spirit, humor, or a special sense of design ... like the women who made them."[6]

Quilt design principles vary with the maker, region, and inspirational fabrics available, but the main principle is to be creative, transfer the design into fabric, and execute it carefully.

IN MY INDEPENDENT STUDY CLASS WITH EMMA SHE HELPED ME collect and make quilts with an eye toward sampling different styles, color schemes, and patterns: to explore design principles for the rest of my life and execute carefully. My first quilt, found in a thrift store, had hundreds of multicolored, one-inch octagonal silk pieces sewn together, in a honeycomb pattern. When I showed it to Emma, she squealed with delight at its detail, but explained it was a labor-intensive design often representing traditional family life in days gone by. For my second quilt I made 30 different types of blocks to explore what I liked, but did not put them together until much later after future life experiences gave me a plan based on life changes. My third quilt had a cotton cover stuffed with feathers from six chickens a neighbor gave me (which turned out to be six roosters who crowed me awake every morning at 6 a.m. for a week). When they started to peck each other to death, a friend and I chopped off each one's head, dunked the still quivering bodies in hot water, plucked the feathers, froze the bodies to eat later, and used the very pokey feathers in my quilt—not a good plan. My fourth quilt made by a friend had large orange and green wool squares with brown borders, and reminded me of each Plateau life zone. My fifth and sixth quilts were made of images from my emerging sense of "place"—prehistoric southwest rock art symbols, a bighorn sheep, flute player, large bird, deer, box-shaped human figures, yucca—appliquéd and stitched into denim blocks, framed, and sewn together.

My next quilt idea was to express my social and political activism in a quilt design, ideas instilled by my parents that led me to protest the Vietnam War, racism, and environmental injustices in high school—passions that later led me to become an advocate for the natural world and open spaces. Emma and I talked about that quilt idea one day after I told her my frustration at seeing wild spaces in Prescott being bulldozed to build trophy houses as second homes. Emma was angry about it too.

"When I was a girl," she cried, "one house was plenty for a whole family. Why do people need two houses? It's a real home and place that makes you happy."

We talked about a possible design—fabric blocks appliquéd with an armed sagebrush, upside down bulldozer, a circle with a slash across a fancy house—and laughed. I told Emma I had read that quilts have been deployed throughout history as instruments of social change. That they can draw you in and shift the conversation, a way for women to gather and have political discourse. I never made this quilt, but may someday.

Emma had many quilts in her museum that expressed her love for her home landscape: Grandmother's Flower Garden, Lemon Star, Vase and Flower Medallion, and the Arizona Commemorative Quilt. There was her copy of the

Ninety and Nine, or Good Shepherd quilt, and her Redwork State Flowers quilt with the official flower of every state. Each time I visited she was dusting, straightening, and examining each of her quilts for damage. She had a strict rule: her quilts were never to be used or sold, only hung on the wall, to stay together for all their lives as part of her family. Family was her "sense of place," so when a woman came into the museum one day and admired one of Emma's quilts and asked if she could borrow it and a couple scrapbooks so she could honor Emma's "family" in a newspaper article, Emma lent them.

Instead, she said, "the quilt and scrapbooks were sold to a museum in Los Angeles. I waited patiently for the return of my family members, but never saw them again," a tear sliding down her cheek.

Emma recorded her quilting life in 15 scrapbooks, as a chronicle of her family. She pasted every letter and article she received from her quilting family in them and carefully inscribed each entry with a date, name, and notation. Postmarked envelopes from each reply were kept; thoughts about her interactions with her correspondents were recorded. She pinned each ribbon she won to the pages, along with the canceled postage stamp from the envelope that delivered it, the needle that made the winning quilt, and a note.

Many travelers stumbled onto Emma's museum, just as I had. Once people found her, they never forgot her, and became part of her family too. When the widow of writer Buckey O'Neill visited, as did cartoonist Reg Manning, and Willis Sower of Rough Riders Troop G, she incorporated stories of them into her window and display cases. Inside one display case was a tiny mouse made from an apple seed, a gift from a quilting friend. Next to it was the thimble she used to sew buttons on Henry Ford's vest. Another display featured gold ore and a miner's candle Emma had found on one of her wagon trips with her Dad. She also kept a single piece of tatting from a friend who was a Canadian convent member and a small carved bell from the household of Czechoslovakian statesman Jan Masaryk, another friend.

One day Barry Goldwater, a friend of Emma's sister, Anna Marcella, happened to drop by the museum and heard her muttering to herself. Anna was an avid follower of politics, and had met Goldwater at a campaign speech in Prescott, where they became fast friends, after which she introduced him to Emma. When he walked into the museum that day, he asked, "Emma, why are you so sad?" She held up her pile of bills and cried, "I don't have enough money to pay these! I used up all my parents' life insurance money after they died to keep the museum afloat." He wrote her a check on the spot that covered what she owed. She gave him a quilt and he was now another member of her extended family.

THIS BLOCK OF MY QUILT WILL BE A BULLDOZER ON ITS BACK, WITH ITS TREADS UP IN THE AIR, AND A SMILING JUNIPER TREE.

Chapter 4

The Idea Fabric

"Color is the dimension of fabric that strikes us first, grabs our attention, and beckons us to take a closer look ... color influences how we react to a particular fabric or quilt."[7]

When you begin a quilt, you must first select a fabric and color scheme that inspire you, called the "idea fabric." From this, all pattern ideas flow.

RESEARCH IN *SCIENTIFIC AMERICAN* MAGAZINE STATES THAT idea fabric for a life starts with a psychological and physical bond between mother and child during gestation. The mother's body supplies the fetus warmth and sustenance, her heartbeat a soothing, constant rhythm, and the fetus' cells migrate through the placenta, integrating into the tissues of the mother's brain (and perhaps hers into theirs) along with cells of her grandmother and great-grandmother.[8] A life full of family stories grows from that very first seedling of an idea.

The idea that became me began when my eventual parents met on a baseball field at the University of Chicago in the summer of 1949. My future dad was playing third base, my future mom shortstop for the International House. The teams were women against men, but there were more men than women, so my dad gallantly volunteered to play with the women's team, telling them it was a "great sacrifice for him." He told my future mom she threw like a girl; she laughed and told him he was out of line.

As a boy, Dad explored being a scientist, once inventing a type of dynamite that blew a streetcar off its track, and the window out of the third-floor of his parents' house. But he found his life calling, as a graduate student in city planning at the University of Chicago, knowing he wanted to be an urban activist, an agent of social change. He saw cities tearing down older housing to build interstate highways, redevelopment projects, and shopping centers; so, he wanted to build affordable housing for families and plan cities based on equality. Mom found her life calling as a drama major at Northwestern University. Her mother had desperately wanted a daughter, after giving birth to three sons. She was ecstatic after her first girl was born, but was told she could not have any more children. When Grandma got pregnant again with my mom, she cried nonstop for the first six months of her pregnancy and handed her off to the nanny as soon as she was born, deeply influencing the psychological and physical bond between mother and child. Living with chronic migraines, she told my mom she was a mistake. So, my mom grew up tap dancing, acting, and telling stories as her path to happiness. And the stage, with adoring fans, did make her happy. She loved being, and was a very popular, "Billy the Brownie" in high school on a Milwaukee radio show that began to appear in Schuster's Department Store advertisements and displays during the 1920s along with Santa Claus and an Eskimo named Metik.

After six months of courtship, when my eventual dad sang to her, "You Are My Sunshine" and "Let Me Call You Sweetheart" and ended with, "*Why don't we just get married*?", she smiled and immediately knew a man who loved her enough to sing to her and make her laugh would make her happy for a lifetime. She said YES!

They married in 1950. My sister came along a year later. Their small family moved to England a few weeks after my sister was born so my father could do independent postgraduate research on British town and country planning and the new national health system. They lived for 18 months on $8,000 and the G.I. Bill, so as to see the world while they were still young and their family small. They traveled to Holland, Germany, France, Austria, Italy, Switzerland, and Israel while my mother was pregnant with me in 1952. I can't help but believe that her emotional experience of this newlywed exploration of the world filtered through to me, so, when I was born in England in November 1952, my mother's spirit of adventure, her pathway to happiness and love, had migrated into my soul at a cellular level, as my idea fabric.

In 1954 my parents both found their political calling in volunteering for Leroy Gore on his "Joe Must Go" campaign while living in Wisconsin. At that time Senator Joseph McCarthy began a witch hunt to ruin politicians' reputations by accusing them, with no proof, of having communist leanings. America, then as now, looked for simplistic answers, was vulnerable to demagogues, and was easily distracted when looking to find solutions to very real problems. McCarthy aimed a wrecking ball at his perceived enemies, and attacked them with fake stories.

Leroy Gore was a newspaper editor in McCarthy's home state of Wisconsin who had become disillusioned with the senator's anti-communist obsession, launched an effort to recall him, and helped coalesce mounting opposition to McCarthy. As their way of standing up to this national bully, my dad was Leroy's chief fundraiser, my mother head of the Mother's March on McCarthy. Joe was censured by the Senate three years before he died of cirrhosis of the liver from severe alcohol abuse. Standing up to bullies became another thread that ran through my life.

In 1959 their family was complete after the birth of my brother, and in 1963 we moved to St. Louis and bought a farm in the Ozarks where we went twice a month to immerse ourselves in whippoorwills, ticks, chiggers, the Huzzah River, copperhead snakes, canoeing, night skies full of fireflies, horses, and red dirt. Dad built a full-size log cabin, then showed me how to square logs and build a log outhouse to match. Log by log, row by row, I added chinking to keep out the breeze of his two-seater. More family scraps for my idea fabric.

I learned Emma's idea fabric and color scheme stories during our long conversations about life and quilting.

Emma's father, Matt, was born in Bavaria and moved to Colorado as a young boy. He met Emma's mother, Anna, in Central City, Colorado, and Matt and Anna married in 1898. They moved to Prescott in 1902, the year Emma was born. Matt opened a cigar store in Prescott and invented 12 brand-name cigars, including Friendship, Santa Fe, No Trust, Solid Comfort, and Casey's Choice. Matt's cigar store produced 7,000 to 8,000 cigars each month, which Matt and Emma delivered by a horse-drawn wagon to the surrounding communities, mostly to miners. Emma's mother was born in Central City, Colorado. In 1895 Anna made a crazy quilt of pieced and appliquéd velvet from various young men's ties, ribbons, and more than $15 worth of silk thread. The small, delicate pieces were embroidered with tiny stitches, with Matt's and her initials at the bottom.

Emma had four siblings, but she was the only child who wanted to work in the cigar store with her father. Her sister Anna entered a convent in California at the age of 15 to become a nun and teacher. When Matt died, Emma converted the cigar store into the Happiness Museum and displayed her devotion to the divine through quilts—like the Good Shepherd quilt—as well as through her letters and museum window displays.

After two of her brothers committed suicide, Emma

had a breakdown and stopped quilting and keeping scrapbooks for a couple of years. She never slept well in a bed again, because she said it made her dream of her brothers, and she took to sleeping on the sofa instead. None of her adopted family would tell me why, just implied there was a story there. Did they commit suicide because of a chemical imbalance, or because of things that happened to them beyond their control? Did Emma dream of them because she knew their dark secrets? All I know is that on the Happiness Museum's wall, she hung a journal entry in her large, loopy handwriting about a photograph in which she saw Christ's face in a tree and a quote about "the Lord is my shepherd, I shall not want.

Our love, family, spirituality, and work helped both of us find our lives' idea fabric and color scheme—that we then chronicled and preserved in cloth.

THIS BLOCK OF MY QUILT WILL BE TWO PARENTS, THREE KIDS, AND A BASEBALL.

Chapter 5

Fabric Selection

....

"When you plan your (quilt) masterpiece, keep the door open for originality and self-expression ... allow yourself to vary your original idea ... Express yourself in this wonderful fabric art."[9]

....

Constructing your own quilt, from fabric selection to bound and finished piece, is a step-by-step process with considerable preparation and thought required.

I THINK FINDING A HOME PLACE IS NECESSARY TO BE HAPPY. Home can be the place where one was born, a place where one likes to be such as the outdoors, a place where one lives, or a place that one discovers and relates to certain happy experiences. For some it is the actual building they live in, or the home of their family or friends. For others, it is wherever their loved ones are, or an internal place, or on a stage singing their truth. Home can really be anywhere, but home for me became a sense of place within a landscape.

As children my sister and I found great joy in catching fireflies with a butterfly net. We ran through our St. Louis neighborhood at night waving nets at clusters of flashing lights, filling them with blinking bugs. We counted each one, put them in jars, then in the refrigerator to keep alive overnight, and in the morning ran to a researcher's house to sell our fireflies for a penny each. He then sold them to the Sigma-Aldrich Corporation who were using the chemicals luciferin and luciferase in the firefly's light (named after Lucifer, the fallen angel of light) for medical research into bioluminescence. This emission of light by a living organism is a source of energy in all living things, and when combined with other chemicals is responsible for many life functions, including the formation of memories. A national network of firefly clubs paid kids like us to collect up to three million of these winged beetles a year. The fireflies blinked no more, unintentionally giving their lives to what scientists considered a more important human need, from disease detection to whether life exists on Mars.

As a teenager lying on the log cabin porch of our Ozark farm, staring out into the blackness of night, I watched many fireflies blink and this time wanted them to live. Blink, blink, blink—like thousands of tiny yellow eyes winking. Were they a specific flashing pattern to signal a desired mate under rotting wood on the forest floor or a patchwork of yellow blinks, tying together an immense fabric of black sky? Or were they tiny sparks of hope, love, reflections, and inspiration tying together the universal cloth of life? Perhaps each firefly was catching a seed of happiness, and tying it into a soul to hold, imagine, and incorporate into a life's fabric. Lying on the porch that night as a teenager, I pondered if I could find a home place where I felt as much love as I did on this farm. Would it involve serendipity or good timing? Good timing is not just a necessity for a sewing machine needle to pick up the bobbin thread below. It's also necessary for ensuring each fabric and color has a "place" in your quilt.

Eons ago, fireflies blinked in the area now called the Colorado Plateau. During those eons the Plateau country was flat and much lower, covered in seas, swamps, and rivers. Over time, dozens of rock layers—limestone, mudstone, sandstone, and shale—were created by pressure and heat on deposits of earth atop these wetlands. Water and wind contributed raw material too—the makings of sandstone layers hundreds of feet thick. The area was thrust upward by forces within the Earth. Colliding tectonic plates tilted and bent the layers like cardboard. Water flowed through the soft stones, carving deep canyons. Now what is visible, through the needlework of time, is what was left behind by the downward erosion of wind and rain—hardened fireflies tacked inside brown sandstone buttes, mud pieced into red rocks, sand woven into rocks the color of bone, tiny sea creatures stitched into gray rocks—all sewn into a patchwork of new landform fabrics. The scissors of time cut up the Earth again and again into different patchworks of landforms and sewed them serendipitously into a **Wild** home place for me.

Through serendipity and good timing I would eventually stitch a joyful life from what I see as five key elements of happiness—*family, love, work, spirituality, humor*—as well as *the six P's of life* (*prior planning prevents piss poor performance*) and *adaptability to inevitable change*; with a sense of *place* pulling it all together. I would learn why I needed to know the acronym for the Plateau's most common rock layers to be happy: Many Canyon Walls Know No Capitalist Exploitation

(Moenkopi, Chinle, Wingate, Kayenta, Navajo, Carmel, Entrada).

Fireflies seemed to have an easier life early on, as did I. But later life did not come as easy for me. In the place I chose to call home, with many two-dimensional unrealistic thinkers, a local right-wing blogger with a following, wrote in the newspaper that the school I would eventually found would be a "rattlesnake breeding den for environmentalists ... there was strong reason to believe it would be used as a staging area for the activities of [Marxist Feminists] groups: closing roads and trails, preventing natural resource development, and in general interfering with the lives of people who live here." I would have to learn from my parents' example how to stand up to bullies.

And yet a supporter of my work said, "she deserves respect because of all she has accomplished, and all she has endured by being the whipping post of everyone who is frightened by change and guided by emotionally charged unsubstantiated falsehoods instead of facts ... she has taken more guff from the misguided of this county than anyone in my memory." And so I would also have to learn to appreciate such friends and love, embrace, and manage it all.

Finding a place to call "home" means different things

to different people. Some have a certain kind of possessiveness about where they were born, as if the location of their birth, or the place where generations of their family have lived, is the only place they can find happiness. And they feel entitled to protect that "place" with all their might. For others joy can be found in any place they choose and want to protect.

Home is also a symbiotic relationship between brain and heart. The brain is central control; it tells the heart what to do and recognizes humor. The heart, the keeper of emotions, sings to the brain and its funny bone to tell it what it wants. Memory formation and the five senses became important in finding home. Memories store away the smell of sagebrush, sight of a favorite view, the touch of a lover, the taste of fresh spring water coming out of red rock, the sound of a canyon wren's descending scale song. Anything that evokes a long, deep body sigh from the heart can tell you that you have found home, as you sense a physical and emotional connection between the heart and brain with cognitive replay. Home is where the heart-brain is, powered by a place.

For each culture a home place has a different meaning—in English home is a place where something flourishes; in French the joy of reuniting with loved ones after a long time apart; and in Fijian the sharing of stories and ideas in order to foster understanding. For me, home has been about the smells, sights, touch, tastes, and sounds—my "senses" of place—on the Colorado Plateau. Finding home often cost me a great deal in time, dollars, and sweat. It had local, global, and psychic costs. But finding home paid me in psychic dividends, environmental benefits, and educational profits. Once I found home my spiritual income exceeded my physical expenses, my life's balance sheet stabilized. Finding "home" for me was fiscally and educationally responsible and paid me with a meaningful and satisfying life's work. Then one day many years later after I found "home," the timing was right, and I too (like Craig Childs in the foreword to this book), "realized I was no longer drifting, but was pacing back and forth across 130,000 square miles of my home ground."

THIS BLOCK OF MY LIFE QUILT IS TEN FIREFLIES, TACKED ONTO A CANYON CLIFF WALL.

Chapter 6

True Bias

"Studying color is not an end in itself; it is simply a means to making better quilts. Once grounded in the fundamentals, you are free to discard stale color schemes, free to flirt with dangerous colors—in short, free to be brave with color (and fabric)." [10]

True bias is when the grain of the fabric is 45 degrees to its warp and weft. When a fabric is cut across the true bias the resulting garment is more elastic and fluid, which varies with fabric type and color.

AS I BEGAN TO FLIRT WITH MORE FLUID IDEAS, NEW OUTDOOR environments and cultures were added to my life bias.

One started in our childhood home in Cincinnati, which was on the edge of the Rawson Woods nature preserve, given to the city by a wealthy family. It stretched across 100 acres, with a creek, and woods dense with buckeye, redbud, maple, and oak trees blanketed with thick green moss. The ground was covered with leaves, and 30-foot vines hung from many trees. My brother, sister, and I raced home from school every day so we could play in the woods until dark. The sweet pungent redbud was overwhelming, we bit off the ends of honeysuckle blossoms to suck out tiny drops of nectar, stepped on dog poop while smelling ginkgo pods in the grass, picked up dark brown shiny buckeyes, swung on vines howling like Tarzan and Jane, and caught crawdads in the creek. I often ran through these woods, pawing the air, fending off an imaginary stallion, rearing up. In my journal I wrote:

Today I am a horse,
tomorrow a cat,
next day a raccoon,
perhaps—
But today I am a horse.
Winds blow my mane
Head shakes of
defiance
freedom

queen of all
that is in me.

Later after moving to St. Louis, I happened to sign up for a non-required high school class in physiography (physical geography) taught by Mr. Poos. I had heard from other students and friends it was a great class if you liked the outdoors and animals. Mr. Poos had learned the word "physiography" from a book he read about John Wesley Powell, who invented the term when he was the director of the U.S. Geological Survey. In 1869, Powell was the first white man to explore and map the physiographic province known then as the Plateau Province, later called the Colorado Plateau. Mr. Poos told our class the story of the rough-and-tumble adventure of this one-armed major, who traveled in a wooden dory for 95 days down 1,000 miles of the Green and Colorado Rivers, hiking its many side canyons before his food stores—some wet and moldy from falling into the river—ran out. I was fascinated by this story and wanted to visit this place.

Mr. Poos took our class to local parks to identify rocks, animals, and flowers. He kept two wild wolves at his house down the street from mine, that he let us observe, teaching us to make scientific notes on the wolves' behavior, interactions, and eating habits. He took us on weekend camping and canoe trips on the Current and Meramec Rivers to study fish and birds. All the other teachers at my school wondered how he could possibly be teaching the curriculum to state standards. I did extra credit projects for him, like feeding his wolves and labeling his rock samples. I asked if he needed help during the summer; if I could be his assistant the following year. He said he had an older student but appreciated my interest. A tear slid down my cheek, but I wiped it away quickly and watched his wolves some more, making notes in my journal.

I told my parents of my disappointment with not being asked to work for Mr. Poos, so they thought it might help me develop a truer life bias if I participated in an Experiment in International Living program with local country homestays and formal school attendance. My sister had experienced international living in Bolivia and later my brother in Yugoslavia, but at 16, I wasn't so sure I wanted to go anywhere. I had the wolves to observe, rivers to canoe, the Vietnam War to stop, women's rights to protect, and rock concerts to attend.

I decided my parents might have a point, I could grow and learn new things, so I chose a six-month experiment in international living with a group of ten girls at Cobham Hall, an English boarding school for upper-class British girls in an old castle in the county of Kent, England, and five boys at a different school. We were required to wear blue and white starched uniforms, and follow lots of rules. If you used the wrong fork at the table, the punishment was jogging down the one-mile driveway and back. If you walked on the grass you were swatted with a cane. It felt like a prison. I found a few students at Cobham Hall, mostly my American mates, who sympathized with my views on civil rights, feminism, and defiance of authority. One British student joined the American girls in our favorite espionage game. After lights out, we slipped out of our rooms and ran through the castle's underground tunnels until we were under the teachers' lounge. Through the cracks in the floorboards, we would listen to the teachers talk about us. "Wow, those American students must be very smart to have been chosen to come to our school," they would say, not realizing we had signed up and paid for this experimental life opportunity. I went to live with the British student at her family's country estate for a month at the end of my stay, and then she came to live with my family for the year following and fulfilled her dream to be an American hippie.

Emma's bias for her life quilt design started with her

correspondence with others who shared her interests in dolls and quilts. Emma had read about Carrie Hall, a ceramic doll maker and co-author of *The Romance of the Patchwork Quilt in America*, in a newspaper in 1932. They never met, yet wrote each other every week for more than 20 years. Every year, Emma purchased more dolls from Carrie, hand-painted from the tips of their hats to the laces on each shoe. One was a lady with a big red hoop skirt and red top, a flowery red hat, button-up black leather shoes that came to her mid-calf, and red fingernail polish and lipstick, somewhat of a likeness to Emma. Another doll made by Carrie looked like Emma's sister Anna, the nun. Emma dusted these dolls daily and never sold them, as they were part of her family.

Emma's quilt pattern bias was from her own outdoor experiences like Lady at the Spinning Wheel, Tiger Lily, Wild Rose, Flower Garden, and Out Where the West Begins. Other quilters use patterns with outdoor names like the Missouri Daisy, Tulips, Rocky Road to Kansas, Dove in the Window, Ocean Waves, and Road to California. My quilts had names like Rock Art of the Southwest, Colors of the Southwest, and Multi Sampler of the Southwest. These life experiences gave Emma's and my quilts an avenue for unique self-expression, a link to our past, and a bridge to our future. I knew my life, like

Emma's, was not going to conform to tradition or convention, nor did I want it to. My life quilt pattern was based on my early brave experiences with family life and the outdoors—my true bias for a happy life.

THIS BLOCK OF MY QUILT WILL BE THE FLAG OF BRITAIN, A BUCKEYE, AND WOLF.

Chapter 7

Background Fabric

"And whether pieced, embroidered, or appliquéd, quilts came to reflect the enduring [perspective] of women. With their profusion of colors, fabrics, and detailed stitchery, quilts can be read as a kind of a textile journal." [11]

In most quilts, a portion of the design serves as the background fabric, a quiet area that helps the rest of the design move forward, so the eye can easily discern the pattern.

MY FAMILY OFTEN FOUND THEIR "HOME" WHEN AWAY FROM OUR actual house. Our first camping trip was exploring the

Ohio and Missouri woods and rivers by foot and canoe and later we explored the wilds of the western United States, in an old blue Rambler station wagon stuffed with sleeping bags, tent, coolers, food, stove, and lanterns. Bags and boxes were tied on the roof, and the back seat had coloring books, songbooks, reading books, blankets, apples, graham crackers, pillows, peanut butter, and bread. Off we'd go, singing "The ants go marching..."

My father often took back roads—gravel, paved, or dirt. Two lanes were all he needed, and to never travel the same route twice. When we passed any historical marker, he pulled over to read it. Every time we passed a log cabin, he slammed on the brakes, and jumped out shouting, "Let's get out and look at it!" Every cabin to him was "a great log cabin" he wanted to have and number the logs, dismantle the cabin, move it somewhere, and put it back together log by log. If he heard of a historic cabin along the way, he'd drive as much as 100 miles out of the way just to see it. We rarely stayed in motels and usually landed by nightfall in our six-foot-high canvas tent. If we did stay in a motel Dad used the opportunity to watch the news. "Everyone be quiet!" he would shout. "I'm listening to the ***NEWS!***"

We jumped on the bed quietly for the news hour and then he would ask us what we had learned. "Not sure, but interesting," I would peep and wiggle into his lap.

"Oh, you goofball," he would croon, smiling and tickling me until I squirmed away.

Except for log cabins and historical markers (*hysterical markers*, he called them), my father never liked to stop; it was a waste of time. This often caused us to go into fits of laughter as we crossed our legs and yelled for a bathroom. On one such trip with our cousin, Norm, our eyes were turning yellow, so we made up a story about Norm's Johns—a national chain of thematic toilets. The "Cowboy John" had a door painted with a cowboy hat, and each toilet bowl was shaped like a saddle, with an appropriate elimination hole in the center. Users would climb aboard using a stirrup and hold the saddle horn, toilet paper in the saddlebags. Later, we invented the BM Museum. It had fresh scat from all animals of the United States in display cases. Each case had captions, histories, and biological descriptions. It was free to get in, but you had to pay to get out. Often with wet cheeks and pants, we would finally arrive at a rest area. Humor was a background fabric in our family! Laughter releases endorphins, enkephalins, dopamine, noradrenaline, and adrenaline, the heartbeat accelerates, blood pressure rises, and vocal cords vibrate. Laughter is triggered by visual, auditory, and tactile stimuli sent to the brain—

byproducts of humorous moments which produce memories.

Throughout my childhood I also had a collection of 50 "wild" plastic and glass horses against my bedroom wall. They were always at the ready to gallop—golden palominos, black stallions, and spotted pintos—ready for ecstasy when they raced across the rug for a few hours, leaping and kicking through the short shag carpet, thus ending their boredom of being not-real. I had a secret fantasy of becoming a **wild** horse someday myself, able to run at will. I longed for a real horse of my own to ride across fields and country roads, a black beauty with a long mane and tail, waiting for me to climb aboard her bare back, responding to my knees and voice with no hesitation, and helping me explore the natural world. "Wild" to me meant an unrestricted exploration of a place, adventurous, and joyful.

When my family bought the farm in the Ozarks, I put my plastic herd away and began lobbying for the real thing. My parents bought me Black Widow, a Missouri Foxtrotter, who was all black except for a small white blaze on her face, with a gliding trot, smooth as a swan landing on water. We pastured her in a neighboring farmer's field. To be able to ride her, I had to first chase her through the pasture for more than an hour. Once I got her into a corner of the field and laid an arm around her neck, she'd stop. Then I'd put on her bridle, jump on her bareback, and head for our farm. Black Widow galloped through the dense hardwood forest with me flat against her neck. When we came to a gate, and I jumped off to open it, getting back on was a trick. Her back feet would circle round and round, while her front feet remained still, like a center pivot on an irrigation system. Once I was aboard again, she took off like a shot. Arriving at the farm, Widow and I rode up the river bottom, swimming its deep pools, splashing through the shallow ones. She was just tame enough and just wild enough for me.

Late one spring day my brother on his horse Smokey, and I on Widow, rode to a Forest Service fire tower five miles away. We climbed the 100 stairs to the top lookout cabin, above the canopies of the trees, and sat kicking our feet back and forth over the edge of the platform.

"I want to play music or run rivers for a living," I told him.

"I want to folk dance or live in another country," he told me.

We broke into a Taj Mahal song, "*Take a giant step ... outside your mind...*" I sang the melody, he the harmony, then a few other songs for an hour, then we climbed down, jumped on our horses, and galloped back to the farm for supper. That evening our mother needed whipping cream from the country store to make ice cream, so I volunteered to ride Widow the seven miles each way to White's "Pleezing" Grocery. I galloped there and back in two hours, and by the time I got back the three pints of cream I carried in my saddlebag were already whipped. We loaded the hand crank machine with it and made chocolate chip ice cream.

The next summer, a friend and I wanted to live at the farm and find jobs. The farm was ten miles from a small, conservative, rural community. We went to the local shoe factory and applied to make shoes. "No jobs," we were told crossly. We went to the local grocery store and applied for a job. "No," we were told again as the owner shut the door in our faces. Finally, we split one job as waitresses for Cobblestone Resort lodge and restaurant. They appreciated our hard-working attitudes and ability to get along with city folk, their main customers. They accepted us, as the city girls we were, and we them.

That fall, my first year at Prescott College, I met a 12-year-old girl who also loved horses. She had a small pony, took riding lessons every day, and rode in shows on weekends. In her room were 40 books about horses, but only one plastic model horse. One night I went out to dinner with her family, and the girl doodled a horse on a napkin. She drew it quickly, but I noticed its lines were fine and captured the image of a horse perfectly.

When I told Emma about this young girl, she exclaimed, "She sounds just like you." That Christmas I boxed up my model horse collection and mailed it to myself in Prescott. When I returned to school, I took the boxes to the young girl's house and left them in her room with a note: "To a horse girl, from a horse woman." Her mother sent me a thank-you note, saying her daughter cried when she got my gift. I told Emma and she smiled and cried a little too, as did I.

Emma told me she began helping her father make and sell cigars in his store part time in 1918. As soon as she finished high school in 1921, she began working in the cigar store full time and learned how to strip tobacco leaves and band cigars. But life got sweeter for her when her father decided to sell magazines, which broke up the monotony of sitting behind the same counter alone day after day. Every Friday after that she anxiously awaited as her father hitched a team of horses to an old wooden wagon. She helped him load dozens of boxes labeled with the name of cigars they contained, then clothes, food, and sleeping bags, just in case they wanted to sleep out. And last they loaded magazines to read by the campfire. Off they traveled for the week to make their deliveries all over Yavapai County, staying with customers, or camping along the way. They dropped off cigars in each town and store, until all the cigars were gone. Then they would head home, laughing and singing, with Emma reading interesting magazine articles out loud as they rode.

"When magazines came, my world started. In the pages of magazines and newspapers I found people and ideas to inspire my work and change my life," she told me.

One day she responded to an ad in a 1931 *Woman's World* magazine, sending for a *Tiger Lily* appliqué quilt kit. She stitched while at work and home, and soon sent for another kit, then another. She began reading news articles about quilt makers and wrote to them, they wrote back, over the years putting every letter and article in a scrapbook.

Our background fabrics were developing, as our lives began to move forward in a high-spirited expressive manner, with humor stitched throughout.

THIS BLOCK OF MY LIFE QUILT WILL BE A LOG CABIN, A TENT, A STATION WAGON AND A BLACK HORSE, WITH A SMALL WHITE BLAZE, RUNNING.

Chapter 8

Contrasting Corners

....

"As much as quilters love purchasing fabric, they are frequently confused when deciding how to use their fabrics ... Some have a knack for combining fabrics and colors to create interesting or unusual combinations." [12]

....

A contrasting color at each corner makes the quilt design work, by picking up a design element, color, or the border itself.

MY PRESCOTT COLLEGE FRESHMAN ORIENTATION GROUP OF TEN students, two instructors, and a professor began with a glider plane flight. In a plane with no engine, but very long wings, we glided silently over the wide Prescott Valley for an hour, which felt, I imagined, like the natural flight of a large bird would. Next was an overnight backpack to Granite Mountain, where we learned basic survival outdoor skills. The final event was a two-week backpacking trip into Dark Canyon and a sea kayak trip down Lake Powell in Utah. The topography included pinnacles, mesas, buttes, spires, and towers of redrock. We started backpacking in the Ponderosa pines in upper Dark Canyon that formed a green piney patchwork on top of layers of tan and creamy white sandstones, gray limestones, and russet red shales. The sandstones were layer upon layer of interbedded rocks varying in color, thickness, and grain size. A fluctuating sea had formed the limestone layers, now exposed as fossiliferous calcium carbonate with crinoids, brachiopods, and bryozoans tacking the rocks together. The endless azure sky, dotted with large white pillows of clouds, hinted at moisture that might be. The landscape that inspired such awe in us would one day become a battlefield between those who wanted to preserve and protect it and those who wanted to exploit its many resources, but right then we were just in awe of the place.

The people on the trip were new to each other and the land. We hiked about eight miles a day with 50-pound packs, walking as slow as the slowest person. We ate granola, peanuts, rice, and lentils for every meal—all-powerful intestinal cleansers. Water sources were often miles apart. We talked late into the night about how tired we were, how gaseous we were, and what we would and would not eat when we got back to school. We never saw another soul until we got to Lake Powell. There we met another group of Prescott College freshmen that had kayaked up the lake, and swapped our backpacks for their kayaks. We paddled for four days before establishing a basecamp for our three-day solo experience. My site was near Castle Butte. I lived under an overhanging rock with only my journal and clothes. It rained hard the first night, but I stayed dry. During the warmth of the day, I made a fishing line out of my shoelaces and a stick; the hook was a safety pin I found in my pocket. All day I wrote in my journal whatever came into my head—about this orientation journey, my fellow students, and the beautiful landscape around me.

When the group reunited after solo, and after eating more gaseous food, I read out loud the story from my journal about being someone named Fanny Fart who lived on Castle "Butt," using her amazing natural gas powers to propel her kayak through a hole in the bottom of the boat. The group added, while also chuckling, that the Air Force should put a plug in my bum to preserve my great powers for future energy needs. We then paddled to Halls Crossing Marina and drove back on the 90-mile dirt road now called Highway 95 to the paved highway U.S. 191. We had become a family. I told my dad on the phone, after I got back to school, I felt like I had been walking toward my destiny, my place, my life mission.

The following summer, after the school year ended, I again went to our Ozark farm. Our neighbor came over, as he often did, for coffee and to chew the political fat with my father. My father was a diehard Democrat, our neighbor a pure Republican. They never agreed on anything when it came to politics, but were fast friends. Our neighbor helped my father re-shingle the roof of his log cabin with cedar shakes and build a blacksmith shop with a cobblestone floor. They walked the fields and talked about the weather and politics. Richard Nixon was president then so there was much to talk about... Our neighbor wanted him to remain president, my father wanted him impeached. The neighbor was amused that my father wanted to return to a time of log cabins, while he worked hard to live in a modern house. They discussed running for president and vice president of the U.S. on a bipartisan ticket, called either Republicrats or Demicans. They thought they could run the country better than past presidents, because they were friends, and could work these things out with humor, making their contrasting views work.

We three worked one day to clean up a pile of old wood. Our neighbor repeatedly warned me, "Be very careful when you pick up a board. There might be a copperhead snake underneath one." When I lifted a board, indeed I did find a copperhead curled beneath, and the neighbor instantly picked up a shovel and cut its head off.

I shouted, "You didn't have to kill him. I was going to scare him off!"

He retorted, "He might have bit you. I was just protecting you. Copperheads can kill you."

"But snakes have a right to live, too," I said, stomping off. An hour later I thanked him, and we were friends again, respecting each other and our contrasting views.

From my dad I learned a love for the outdoors, the importance of finding a life calling, and understanding the bonds that tie all living things together are deeper than the superficial alliances of politics. He believed that laughter and finding the best in everyone can be the shortest distance between two brains and build an instant social bond.

THIS BLOCK OF MY QUILT IS A BACKPACK, BLACKSMITH ANVIL, AND A COPPERHEAD SNAKE.

Chapter 9

Pattern Preparation

....

"Women have always made special quilts to commemorate notable personal events ... When we read these chronicles in cloth, we discover the history of individuals, families, and communities, written with thread." [13]

....

Planning your quilt pattern well, before cutting the cloth, is essential to a high-quality finished product.

AN EARLY LIFE PATTERN PREPARATION OF MINE BEGAN AT TEN years old when I was smitten with a boy, but too scared to tell him. I had gone to Camp Talaki that summer in Wild

Rose, Wisconsin, a YWCA camp where we canoed and fished daily. I expressed my feelings to this boy by mailing him two fish eyeballs wrapped in red tissue paper, tied at the top with a bow. When I returned from camp, he chased me around the house, caught me, pulled me into a room, and kissed me hard on the mouth. I ran out of the room, and never saw him again.

The second time I was intrigued by a boy I was 17. He was 20 and a banjo player. We often went caving and hiking, especially at our family farm. He was my introduction to bluegrass music, whose tempo and rhythm patterns first grabbed my attention and held it firm. He plucked, slid, and rolled those strings as fast as he plucked my heart. He taught me to sing, while he harmonized, to a song by Badger Clark and Clifton W. Barnes, "Cowboy's Lullaby": *"Desert silvery blue in the pale moonshine..."* Musical patterns connected us to the natural world. Music's tempo and rhythm mimicked the extreme ranges of our human heartbeats—50 to 200 beats per minute—relaxing at the low end, energetic at the high end. With him I perceived higher notes as light yellow and happy, lower notes bluer and ominous.

Years later I met another boy on a Prescott College trip to climb the San Francisco Peaks near Flagstaff, Arizona. Later he wrote poetry and songs about me and walked nine miles at night for a secret rendezvous in my dorm. He took me to a restaurant called The House of Joy. He climbed a 14,000-foot peak in Colorado and wrote me a love poem at the top. I was enchanted by his passion for life, the desert, and his obsession with me. Later he and I went to Oregon by hopping freight trains. We first hitchhiked to Los Angeles and approached a brakeman to ask when the next train was headed north.

"The Zipper will be along real soon," he said. "Go to a cross street in town, 'cause they slow down there, and jump on. Good luck!"

A train full of piggyback cars, three layers high and full of automobiles, approached our cross street an hour later. As it passed, we threw our packs on and jumped quickly aboard, climbing to the highest layer. We found a Cadillac Seville with its doors unlocked and kicked back in quiet, shock-absorbed comfort for our ride up the California coast.

On the way home a week later, we asked a yardman which train was headed south. "I'm making up a southbound train right now," he cheerily replied, "and I'll put an empty train car on for you. Then I'll pull it by real slow, so you can practice jumping on. Y'all snuggle up in there, you hear?" We rode the train for the next 36 hours without sleeping, through the Feather River Valley and on south, sitting on a small stack of plywood that cushioned us from the intermittently jolting ride. Looking out the rectangular freight car door that framed the movie screen of our visible world we watched a continuous, never-ending reel of yellow silk sun, green wool trees, and crystal blue sky fabric roll out before us. He serenaded me with a Jimmy Rogers bluegrass song, *"When it's peach pickin' time in Georgia, it's gal picking time for me."* I loved the song and its yodel refrain, but wondered if he really was picking me, and me him?

We spent the next winter hitchhiking to visit each other between Prescott, Arizona and Silverton, Colorado, where he was teaching backcountry skiing. One weekend, I decided to surprise him, so I asked his friend to drop me off as close as she could to his cabin. I had refused her offer of skis, even though six feet of soft snow blocked the ¾ mile trail to his cabin. I sank to my waist as soon as I left the road, so I tried crawling, then made snowshoes out of old boards I found at the base of a tree, tying them to my boots with my shoelaces. Six hours later, I was within shouting distance of his cabin. He had just come outside to chop wood and heard me yelling. He skied over to see who it was. When he saw me with boards tied to my feet, sweating, wearing a pointed Peruvian llama hat, he fell down laughing. About six months later he sent me a letter from his travels to Peru, with three lines from a traditional song "The River is Wide." I cried as I read:

Love grows old
And waxes cold
And fades away like the morning dew

Emma's life pattern-making was deeply influenced by a family who moved to Prescott. The wife, an amateur quilter, and her husband, an auto salesman, stumbled into the Happiness Museum. Emma asked them to fix its back door, as it was off its hinge. Soon they were fixing anything that was broken in her museum, buying her hats, taking her to the doctor. Later they remodeled her house when it was condemned by the city, bathed her when she was too old to get in and out of the tub alone, helped her water her plastic "flower garden," and bought her large red hats with plastic roses on top. They fixed the car she named Hazel, let her sleep at their house all night on the sofa, and made her Christmas dinners. She became a grandmother to their three children, baking cakes to celebrate each child's birthday. This family had not planned to stay in Prescott forever, but once they met Emma, they loved her immediately and could not leave her. Sitting with her until midnight, they often helped her go to sleep by listening to her tell her favorite stories, most often of the last person hung by the neck in Prescott. Her adopted family promised they would be her family forever.

Her blood family, her nephews, said to her, "Move to Phoenix, so we can take care of you. There's a great care facility, you can live near us, you won't have to wear those crazy hats anymore, and we can dress you like our 'Scottsdale Grandma.'" But Emma had a Happiness Museum in Prescott full of quilts she had to care for, and did not want to move. She had worked hard to ensure that the materials, craftsmanship, and design of the quilts she made were works of art, so if the color of the thread did not match the fabric, she dyed it the right color. If the fabric was not appropriate for the theme of the quilt, she ordered some from a catalog. She read hundreds of quilting articles every year and asked questions of fellow quilters to be sure her designs and craftsmanship were the best. She entered her quilts in shows and exhibitions and often donated the money she won to a place she had read about and liked the mission of, Father Flanagan's Boys Town. "You can't pick your family, but you can pick your friends," she said.

Louisa Kline, a German girl Emma met, had made a

quilt in 1942 that Emma later bought, with four red hearts and four red roses, and shortly thereafter she became engaged. Louisa had not heeded an old superstition: never use hearts on a quilt before you are actually engaged, or bad luck will come. On her wedding day, everyone came to the wedding but the groom. Louisa never saw him again. So she sold the quilt to Emma who then had a courtship by letter with a widowed needle-worker in Colorado whose work she admired. They exchanged letters for more than two years. Her heartfelt letters preserved in her scrapbooks showed she cared for him, and his heartfelt letters she saved hinted he was going to propose to her. She quilted some hearts on a piece of fabric and waited for the actual words. Then his letters suddenly stopped, and her letters to him were returned. Emma suffered a breakdown. For a year, she didn't make quilts or write letters. One day she read in a newspaper that her widower had died suddenly of a heart attack a year earlier. Emma mourned, but she began to quilt again.

Do a pattern of correspondents, adventures, and humorous experiences, while colorful, make a loving partner relationship work for the long or even short term? Or are they just memories encoded in sensory areas of the brain, stored in file folders to examine later? Locked in this time, frozen forever, these life experiences, for Emma and me, are essential elements of our life pattern preparations.

THIS BLOCK OF MY QUILT WILL BE TWO FISH EYEBALLS, A BANJO, A LETTER, AND A TRAIN.

Chapter 10

Sets

....

"Memories ... become more and more precious as we grow older ... one reason why ... quilt collecting has undergone a tremendous surge in popularity ... what could better help bring warmth and permanence to your home than a quilt?" [14]

....

Sets are groups of blocks arranged in a pattern on a quilt top. Memorable, well-designed sets are the first step to quality design and workmanship in a quilt, creating warmth and permanence.

WHAT HAD ATTRACTED ME TO PRESCOTT COLLEGE IN THE FIRST place was a curriculum that included hiking, camping, rafting, and rock climbing—all leading to a degree in outdoor education, not a common career choice back then. I had been told by many adults that to be a grownup you needed to work for a living, that fun happened after work. Working as an outdoor educator, I thought, would be too entertaining, too lightweight, so it must be a "pretend" job. I asked Emma if my soon-to-be chosen profession was a real job.

"I made my living, after my father died, running a Happiness Museum," she countered. "Is that real work?"

"I think you would be lucky if you get to work at what you loved, as my dad did," I sighed.

"Agreed," she said, smiling. "Nothing wrong with enjoying your work."

I started finding lots of ads for outdoor jobs in newsletters and magazines, that seemed like fun and provided a living wage like:

1. Wanted: Backpack instructor—must have good back and bad book.
2. Wanted: Fire tower attendant—must have many good books and want to write one.
3. Wanted: Backcountry ranger—must be able to range widely in the backcountry and hike all day long and eat gaseous food.

4. Wanted: River guide—must be able to row a boat, drink beer all day, tell dumb jokes, and never take a bath.

At first, I assumed a job as an outdoor educator meant I had to be a 5.10 rock climber, Class 10 boater, or Mount Everest high-altitude climber. By the time I graduated from Prescott College, I knew otherwise. After graduation I got my first "real" outdoor education job at a wilderness therapy program called Darrow Hall/Operation Breakout, a 42-day intense outdoor immersion experience for inner-city St. Louis and Chicago juvenile delinquents. It was run by the Christian Brothers, and based two hours outside St. Louis in their former retreat center.

My first assignment the day I arrived was to remove several 200+-pound limestone statues of the Virgin Mary that had been placed in grottos throughout the property. The brothers thought the statues might intimidate the troubled youth who went to contemplate there, so I spent my first work day with other staff removing statues, pushing them off a cliff to shatter, and moving the pieces by wheelbarrow to a ditch for burial. Clearly, this job was not going to be religiously based, which was fine by me, as I considered myself an atheist, or at least an agnostic.

I imagined working with teenage delinquents was

going to be a challenge. I had been trained in outdoor skills in college, but the program trained us in Transactional Analysis, a psychoanalytic theory and method of therapy. I was not sure its non-judgmental, non-religious philosophy of "I'm OK, You're OK" (a tenet of transactional analysis and primary operating ideology of the camp) would work well for these kids, since they had to return home where single mothers and absent fathers who had hung themselves in prison were more the norm. It seemed technical outdoor skills had some use here; compassion and therapeutic skills more.

The retreat center itself was challenging after a nun was allowed to move in, who locked herself in a room, covering its walls with silver foil and telling the brothers she needed to write a book about how the Jewish Freemasons were taking over the world. She chanted loudly much of the night in her room, scaring the kids and the outdoor staff (some of whom were Jewish and quite offended). She never came out during the day, but during one of her nightly food patrols, she told a staff member that almost anyone could be a Jewish Freemason (even a squirrel), and if they touched your solar plexus it could be fatal. Other than that she allowed no one to talk to her. Six months later, after the outdoor staff begged the brothers to get her out, they brought in the local sheriff to break down her door. When she came after the sheriff with a big kitchen knife, he arrested her.

Youth were sent by state agencies as an alternative to incarceration, some were even wards of the state; none had chosen to be there. Each six-week session included two weeks of backpacking and rock climbing, two weeks of canoeing, and two weeks on a final expedition. In one session, two kids started a 30-acre forest fire. In another, a boy wet his sleeping bag every day for two weeks, washed it out, then carried this 20-pound wet cotton sleeping bag for a full day on top of his 30-pound pack, refusing to wring out the water. In another session we found the kids were burying all their trash instead of carrying it out as required, and another group were throwing rocks at squirrels and killing them. Most of the groups were all boys, but I did work with one all girls group. Two of the girls were inspired to join the military after the course and from the follow-up I heard it changed their lives for the good.

The final expedition of one of our six-week sessions one March was a ten-day backpacking expedition in Zion National Park. One section of the hike required us to rappel into a slot canyon, and swim through a 30-foot-long, deep, and very cold pool of water called the black hole. With a rope to move an inner tube back and forth and lay our packs on, we swam through one at a time, pushing our packs ahead of us. The others would pull the tube back upstream and follow the same procedure. Leaving the other instructor with the group, I told him I would swim through the pool and build a fire about 300 yards down canyon in an open area so each new arrival could dry out and warm up. Everyone except for one of the kids and my co-instructor came through the black hole and sat by the fire. After a long wait, my co-instructor finally came stumbling to the fire. Shivering, he jumped into his sleeping bag, pulling the top up tight over his head. "What happened?" I asked, but he didn't answer. I walked up the canyon and found a cold, still body near the pool. I felt for his pulse and found none. I ran back to the fire and pulled at my co-instructor's bag, whispering, "What happened?"

He climbed out of his bag and walked away from the group, motioning for me to follow. He had seen this boy swim before, but this time he was terrified by the cold, dark water of the slot canyon, and balked at swimming across. He had started across and returned three times. The instructor took his pack across, gently tried to talk him out of his fears, as we had rappelled into a slot canyon and had to go through to get out. On his fourth attempt, the boy went down. The instructor dove for him, pulled him out, and started cardiopulmonary resuscitation, but he could not revive him, his airway was blocked. He tried to open the boy's airway again and again and again to breathe life back into him, but it was blocked and nothing he did would open it. After 45 minutes my co-instructor, shivering uncontrollably, gave up or he would have died of hypothermia himself, and limped to the fire to warm up.

He told me privately, and we decided to tell the other boys as best we could, what had happened. They went totally silent. As a group we decided we could not carry him out both physically and emotionally, and to leave the body in a safe place inside a sleeping bag in respect and come back for it with help. We hiked out in about 20 hours and called the National Park Service. Two rangers and my co-instructor went back and retrieved the body; I stayed with the students. My co-instructor and I called the program administrators who begged the local coroner for an autopsy to determine if drugs had played any part in this death. It was very possible in this program that the boy had snuck drugs into his pack. The coroner refused to conduct it—probably because the boy was Black, and this was Utah in the 1970s. Dying while Black was real then too. My co-instructor and I were very sad and angry at the coroner, and too young to insist it happen or think about filing charges, and the program administration did not insist either.

His body was returned to his parents for burial; they were devastated. They knew he was a good swimmer, and could not figure out why he panicked. They were paid $25,000 as a liability claim. When we returned to the retreat center I knew I did not want to work with this population anymore. It scared me, even though I understood that wilderness therapy might really help these youth and could be meaningful. I was not the right person for the job, and back then adequate training was not provided or required. I had to ask myself, were we somehow guilty of not doing everything we could for his safety, was this just a freak accident, had he snuck drugs into his pack, what could we have done differently? Outdoor industry safety and training standards were lacking in the 1970s. While we did have first aid training, it was not common knowledge then that if a person swallowed cold water their larynx would spasm, thus cutting off their airway. I would learn later that a simple Heimlich Maneuver was the fix, and would open the airway, but did not know that at the time. We had a tiny bit of training in Transactional Analysis, but were not required to be certified as a Wilderness Therapy program, as such programs are now. There were many questions left unanswered and I would just have to live with that.

The program continued for a few more years. In 1980 I read in a St. Louis newspaper:

A wide range of youth in (juvenile offender programs), have reported 15 deaths in 17 years while serving about 70,000 students in the 1970s. But none of about 50 other outdoor programs for juvenile offenders in the United States and Canada has reported anything more serious than broken limbs, wilderness educators say. In sharp contrast, Operation Breakout had six fatalities in three incidents in a six-year period from 1973 to 1979 while serving about 1,000 youths... And questions of poor judgment, weak administration and inadequate safety planning by Darrow Hall have been raised by professional analysts and former staff members. Outdoor adventure programs are designed to improve the skills and self-confidence of urban-oriented Americans. Participants hike, camp, climb, canoe and participate in other activities that test their physical and psychological abilities to survive in the wilderness. For juveniles who think they're "losers," wilderness courses are said to produce a new sense of self-worth that results in improved behavior...

Experts made recommendations for improved

administration, some were made. Despite these tragedies, Darrow Hall survived a few more years, even after the four fatalities in 1979. Wilderness educators, court officials, former staff members and others cite the following reason: The program works. Like other such programs, Operation Breakout has been effective in reforming juveniles, officials said. Although no studies had been done on all participants, limited analyses show that benefits compare favorably with other longer and more costly methods. Some risks are inevitable. Wilderness courses involve risks that never can be completely controlled, the experts say. Planning can minimize but not prevent danger.

Later a social worker from Chicago did an "off the books" unofficial survey of Operation Breakout outcomes and determined that the delinquent youth in this program, whose lives we sought to change, re-offended at a considerably lower rate than those whose therapy was based in an institution.

I now knew working for a boot camp for troubled teens was not what I wanted to do for my life. Sense of place or appreciation of place cannot be mandated or forced, it must be desired, intentionally sought, and nurtured. I wanted to work with groups of people who appreciated wild places, wanted to be there, care for, and protect them, and I needed different and adequate training for that path and that audience. This part of my series of outdoor education jobs did not feel like avoiding maturity or entering a frivolous career; it was engaging, often challenging work. It would inspire me to start an outdoor education school focused on place, with people who loved that place, and whose lives and careers would be improved by a sense of that place, even though it too would have difficult elements. Learning what my life mission truly was, brought me a feeling of warmth and permanence.

THIS BLOCK OF MY QUILT WILL BE A BACKPACK AND A VIRGIN MARY STATUE.

Part Two

HUMOR PIECES A LIFE QUILT TOGETHER

"Rich, meaningful relationships exist among quilts, quiltmaking, and landscape ... Landscapes influence quilts and quiltmaking ... We recognize implicit connections between landscape and (quilts) when we borrow (quilt) terms to describe human manipulation of the land and the resulting patterns." [15]

Chapter 11

Seam Ripper

·········

"There is nothing so wonderful as your first quilt, big or small ... It is like a first child ... it is special. Your heart will always be in your first quilt. Never give it away from the family. It is a work of love—your work and your emotions." [16]

·········

A seam ripper is a small, hand-held implement used to undo stitches that you do not want as part of your quilt pattern.

AFTER MY FIRST YEAR OF COLLEGE IN OREGON, THAT SUMMER I went on an adventure with my Wilderness class teacher. He had gotten a job working on a logging crew near Wrangell, and I was instantly drawn to this place. I was just beginning to explore what "a place" meant to me, and not sure how Alaska fit into my need for a place. Over the following years I spent six consecutive summers exploring the vast green wild landscapes of Alaska with its 220 inches of rain a year, thinking it might be my landscape love, my key to happiness as it were.

I drove to Seattle in mid-August, and just before dark boarded the Alaska Marine Highway ferry. I laid out my sleeping bag, ate a sandwich for dinner, and fell asleep listening to the rain on the deck cover above me. In the morning, the deep green sea rolled in gentle swells just off shore. Gray dolphins led the ship north like small strapless tugboats, each jumping over a wave, screeching, then diving down and back up again. The sun peeked through the clouds, pointing one thin ray on a glacier that came down to the water's edge, like a large white tongue lapping at its ocean bowl. It was about 60 feet thick near the water with crevasses that appeared to be at least 80 feet thick further up. Each time a wave from our wake hit the glacier's front edge it cracked and slowly broke off. When a chunk of blue ice fell in the ocean, it sent a wave toward our ship. The ice bobbed up and down in its giant ocean cocktail until it came to rest with only a small amount of its entire mass above the water's surface. An orca breached the surface; its enormous black-and-white body came straight up from the water, like a giant exclamation point. Dolphins swam around the whale, and one jumped right over its great tail, as if they were dancing together. Hundreds of Sitka Spruce and shore pines bordered the glacier. Each stood straight and tall, of equal height, like whiskers on the face of the Earth. Gigantic mountains were lounging in the distance, some as high as 18,000 feet above the ocean's surface. Rock, ice, and snow covered these silent beings, like knobby knitted caps. A moose came to shore and stared at the boat, water dripping from its muzzle. A bear approached the water, grabbed a fish, and lumbered back into the woods. I slept only after dark. At this latitude in August, it was only dark from midnight until 5 a.m., so the rest of the time I watched an orgy of fish, trees, ice, snow, mosquitoes, bears, and moose.

I met my boyfriend in Wrangell, Alaska. We left on the ferry the next day after we met up, and traveled up the coast to Sitka, Juneau, Haines and then Skagway. From there we hitchhiked north to Denali National Park and later to the Yukon, leaving the rain behind, but not the mosquitoes. Each night we slept in our tiny tent. When it was clear enough, we saw the northern lights—sheets of green, blue, red, and orange shimmering in waves across the sky. After three weeks of travel north, we turned back south, hitchhiking 1,400 miles of the Alcan Highway.

The next year I fished with a friend from Prescott College on a salmon packer near Ketchikan. He lent me a wetsuit to go diving one day and I caught a baby octopus. I cooked a different dish from each of its eight legs, stuffed the round body with vegetables and meat that I boiled for hours, and used its ink to write my parents a letter. On a long walk into a small town, I found a bar that featured a phone booth inside an upright coffin. I called my parents and said, "Having a wonderful time, but calling you from my coffin." Was fishing calling me away from the love of my idea of an Alaskan home?

That summer I had met a couple in Ketchikan who invited me to work with them at the BS Trading Post in Port Protection, on the north end of Prince of Wales Island, the next year. I spent that summer working for them and fishing in a small skiff with an 80-year-old native fisherman named Flea. He had a trawling line off the back of his boat, and every time he baited his hook, he spit tobacco juice on the bait. He always caught more fish with bait and tobacco juice than I did with just bait on a rod and reel. One day after a long cast, my pole jiggled then bent to the sea. As I slowly reeled in my line a giant salmon rose to the surface, just barely hooked in the gill. Flea looked over at my fish and yelled, "It's asleep!" and gaffed it quickly into the floor of the boat. The fish awoke and started fighting, rocking the boat violently as Flea laughed and laughed, then rapped it once on the head, killing it. I hated that, but when we got to the cannery it weighed in at 38 pounds, and they paid me $56. Again, was fishing calling me to leave this Alaskan home?

Back in Port Protection I applied to homestead a small piece of Forest Service land. I drew up a house plan and submitted it to the Forest Service. On getting my approval papers, I now had five years to build a house, which gave me time to think about what my plans and this place really meant. The only way to get to this island was by personal boat, floatplane, or a mail boat that came every two weeks. Only 25 people lived full time in Port Protection, all of them hermits. I had no money to buy tools or pay for help and no partner. The Forest Service had just let contracts for logging 50 percent of the trees on Prince of Wales Island over the next ten years. I had no boat and no experience in conventional long-distance ocean travel. About 220 inches of rain fell every year, it was dark more than 18 hours a day for six months of the year, and it was very far from family and friends. I decided maybe I was not meant to build a home here, and let the land revert back to the federal government.

My next summer in Alaska I canoed for six weeks from Sitka to Glacier Bay National Park and then to Juneau with five other people, about 200 miles along the west coast of Chichagof Island and then about another 60 miles to Juneau. We paddled hard, weaving in and out of islands protecting us from big ocean swells, while it rained almost every day. Bears explored our camps, eating berries and more berries. Before we left the mainland, we had shipped food to post offices in villages along the way for resupplies. En route we visited White Sulfur Hot Springs, where I curled up in the warm water and dreamed of a warmer sun and no rain.

The next two summers I worked as a backcountry ranger for the Klondike Gold Rush National Historical Park in Skagway Alaska, its first year as a National Park and my first real outdoor education job. My two female co-workers and I lived at Sheep Camp, 13 miles from the trailhead at Dyea, and 20 miles from our headquarters in the town of Skagway. We lived in two canvas wall tents, one a sleep tent the other a cook tent, plus an outhouse and sauna. A small bat we called Icarus lived with us, crawling out the ridgepole of the sleeping tent each night to hunt, and returning by daylight to sleep above our oil heat stove. We called our camp the Devil's Club, after a very common plant in southeast Alaska with spines and stinging hairs—an important plant in traditional contemporary Native American/First Nations cultures throughout the Pacific Northwest, used for a broad variety of things, from fishhooks and lures to charcoal as a base for tattoo ink. Bears would wander by the Devil's Club ranger camp looking for blueberries and fishing for salmon in the nearby Taiya River.

Our ranger job, following in the footsteps of the 1898 Gold Rushers, was for one of us to hike every day 3.5 miles and 2,000 feet elevation gain one way up and over the Chilkoot Pass into Canada to ensure the safety of visiting hikers. One day I carried an ice cream maker and a small backpack stove to the small Canadian A-frame shelter near the top. On warm days I would make ice cream for hikers, using the perpetual snow on the summit of the pass; on cold days I would make tea or soup. Every afternoon on the way back to Sheep Camp, when there was still snow on the pass, I would slide down 1,000 feet on my butt with an ice axe at hand for stops. After dinner one of us would walk to the hiker cabin about half a mile away and tell Gold Rush stories to hikers who were to climb the pass the next day. In total over the two seasons I worked there I hiked the Chilkoot Pass about 130 times, and came to love every inch of it—but not as a home base.

Alaska showed me how a landscape, its diverse people, and wildlife, could influence the pattern of my life. Alaska allowed me to expand my worldview of the importance of "place." But, even after six seasons of exploration, and experiencing my first love of a place, Alaska was a lover with whom I could not stay. I ripped out my soggy Alaska stitches, knowing this was not the final pattern of place for me. I needed to remake my blocks of "place" so my life quilt would hold together.

THIS BLOCK OF MY LIFE QUILT WILL BE A MAP OF THE GREAT STATE OF ALASKA.

Chapter 12

Quilting Bees

....

"Quilt(s) endowed a handcrafted piece of needlework with personal meaning and were inspired by a wide range of experiences. Religion ... nature ... were all reflected in thousands and often lyrical pattern names." [17]

....

Long ago, women held quilting bees to celebrate special events and people, or just to get together and share news and diverse ideas, traumas, and joys over the finishing of a quilt.

NEXT I BEGAN TO SHARE DIFFERENT WILD PLACES WITH OTHERS in my continuing exploration of finding my place, each a quilting bee of sorts.

Quilting Bee News Bulletin: First was Wyoming's Greater Yellowstone ecosystem, with 34,375 square miles of wilderness and wildlife. It was home to America's first national park, a land of wild mountain ranges, hot springs, snowcapped peaks, herds of bison and elk, and meadows of tall green grass with purple, blue, and yellow wildflowers—not quite as isolated from family and friends.

My introduction to Yellowstone was as a student on a two-week course run by the National Outdoor Leadership School (NOLS—based in Lander, Wyoming). Our Yellowstone in Winter course curriculum was to share diverse natural wonders (hot springs, wildland, wildlife, and mountains) with 20 like-minded people. We shared news daily—temperatures of ten below zero, 70-pound packs, ten feet of snow to ski through from the south entrance of the park around the 50-mile Heart Lake loop.

Yellowstone has more geysers and hot springs than anywhere in the world—about 2,000. They were formed when surface water seeped deep into the Earth, was superheated by magma, and rose back to the surface, creating an ecosystem that featured animals and plants that thrive in hot water. In a set of concentric rings, fungi live in the hottest water (140 degrees Fahrenheit), while true algae favors 132 degrees, protozoa 122 degrees, invertebrates 117 degrees, ephydrid flies 109 degrees, higher plants 104 degrees, and vertebrates 100 degrees. The tiny ephydrid fly, which lives only two weeks, can surround itself in a bubble to venture into much hotter water to feed on microorganisms. Other animals eat hot water lovers, like spiders, dragonflies, tiger beetles, wasps, and killdeer, a macro-micro quilting bee of hot water life!

Three years later as a NOLS instructor, I led another trip of 20 like-minded people into Yellowstone in winter. This time we shared the natural world of above zero temperatures and rain, again with ten feet of wet snow, and 70-pound packs. We came to a river, high from all the previous day's rain and snowmelt, and took off our clothes to wade across. Three at a time, holding hands for balance and wearing nothing but boots, we crossed the waist-deep water. I could not feel my feet or legs by the time I reached the opposite shore, but I put my clothes on clumsily and ran around in circles to warm up. After skiing to camp a half-mile away where others had made hot drinks, I opened my pack and found that all the matches inside a bag had lit, melting all my plastic food bags together. Nothing was now edible. I went to borrow some food and found one of our group members stumbling around in the snow. His eyes were glassy, and he couldn't speak. I shared this news with others who helped me put him in a tent, take off his clothes, and put him in a sleeping bag with another student to share body warmth. We fed him hot chocolate and within an hour, he was talking and laughing again. Sweet news!

On all NOLS courses we were taught to use the six P's of life philosophy: prior planning prevents piss poor performance. The six-P's were part of the NOLS dogma, along with "Earl," a term for the all-powerful force that controls the weather and other events. "Earl's mad," we often said. "You better practice the six P's tonight: never put your matches in a bag where they can rub together, tie your tent down, or Earl will blow your camp away."

Many years later, one year after 14 wolves were reintroduced to the park, I began to co-lead wolf-watching trips in the park with a well-known naturalist and tracker. We even watched some wolves that had been trapped in Canada, and released into the park. The park was officially wolf-free from 1924-1935, yet wolves had strayed in by the 1990s. The prey base for them was now healthy: 16,000 elk, 600 moose, and 800 bison. Other top predators fought them for prey, including about 121 mountain lions, 20 wolverines, and 200 grizzly bears. My co-leader explained, "The Park Service believes that conservation and protection of its natural resources should happen naturally, without the interference of man." By 2004, the park had a viable wild population of 238 wolves. Groups of wolf watchers, including mine, would drive all day up and down the Lamar Valley—home of the Druid, Rose, and Swan Lake Packs—stopping to ask for information when they saw clusters of people with spotting scopes sharing park news. We all talked in "wolf watcher's language."

"Have you seen Number 238?" someone would ask excitedly of another group on the road.

"Not today, but we did see U Black do an RLU (raised leg urination) by the road," I offered. "Did you hear that Number 106 possibly denned this year?"

"No, but I heard that Number 100 had pups by Alpha 21. Isn't that cool! And there's a kill over by Soda Butte that Rose Creek is feeding on." We drove to see for ourselves as our daily celebration of special wolf events or just to get together and share wolf news.

<u>Quilting Bee News Bulletin:</u> On another NOLS course in lower Dark Canyon, we had been out for two weeks with 60-pound backpacks and had two more weeks to go. Toward the end of a 15-mile day hike to explore a side canyon and learn about rock layers, one of the students stepped off a ledge too quickly, landed hard on her ankle, and heard a small pop. Earl was testing us, I thought. Her ankle began to swell immediately, so we carried her over to a small pool of cold water where she soaked her ankle as we ate lunch. One student took her daypack, while two others formed a chair with their interlocked arms, and we

moved her slowly back to camp. We discussed how to proceed, as we were 20 miles from a paved road at the bottom of a 1,200-foot canyon. We had been trained in the six P's, so we would have to use our improvisational skills to get her out.

About an hour later, we heard a helicopter. It circled and then landed near the stream 200 yards away. I realized quickly if I ran over to the chopper and asked maybe they would fly her out.

"Where are you headed?" I queried out of breath.

"We're taking water samples to decide if this is a good place for a nuclear waste repository. We stopped for a water sample and have to get more samples today before dark," he replied.

"We have an injured student, maybe a broken ankle. Can you fly her out?" I asked.

"Sure, young lady. But you will have to accompany her, and we have a few more stops to make before we land in town."

"Just let me pack up my stuff," I said.

The student and I climbed into the helicopter and we took off. The rest of the day we flew all over Canyonlands, landing three more times for water samples. I was mesmerized by the earth fabric below of red, white, brown, and beige spires, hoodoos, and mesas poking up, bordered by sinuous river strips of riparian green and occasional random blocks of snow-covered mountains with a background of blue sky. They dropped us off at the local airport just as darkness fell, and a friend came and took us to the hospital.

The next day, after ten x-rays and the doctor scolding her for being out backpacking instead of at home making babies, the student got a full leg cast for a tiny crack in her ankle. She burst into tears when he told her she could not finish her three-month-long semester course. I whispered into her ear, "Just ask for your x-rays and when you get back to Lander, go to another doctor for a second opinion. He will probably remove the cast, put on an ankle brace, and let you finish after a few weeks of rest." She smiled then. While waiting three more days for the NOLS bus to retrieve us, and the rest of our group, she and I talked.

"Did they say they might put a nuclear waste dump near Dark Canyon?" she asked.

"Yes. The people in the helicopter said they were exploring that possibility," I answered. "I have heard talk about that and read some news stories too."

"How could they do that to such a spectacular landscape? They would have to build roads and offices, with lots of radioactive truck traffic, and it would never be the same. It could poison local communities' water sources and food production. I have read that this area has a long history of cancer caused by people being downwind from nuclear bomb testing in the 1940s. They are not thinking about the six P's now, are they?"

"I agree and am glad you read that. I hope you use that information in the future wisely," was all I could say. Turned out to be a forecast of this and other land conflicts to come.

Quilting Bee News Bulletin: I soon planned a private trip back to Utah with some NOLS friends to look for land to buy as a NOLS canyon country basecamp. I was thinking this was going to be my "place." I had read *Desert Solitaire* by Ed Abbey recently, just finished his *Monkey Wrench Gang,* and looked up Abbey's phone number in Moab. I called him and asked if I could visit, as he was a guru for many desert lovers and environmentalists, and perhaps me too.

"Sure, young lady, come on out to my house," he said, and gave me directions. My friend and I knocked on the door of his small, ramshackle house at the edge of town surrounded by prickly pear cactus, rice grass, and sage-brush. Inside, a picture window with a view of Behind the Rocks, an area of magnificent redrock fins and canyons, framed a gray-haired man with a beer belly. He gestured toward the couch. We told him we loved his books and shared his environmental views.

"I'm no environmentalist," he said. "I throw my beer cans out the window all the time. I think if I throw enough out, all the people will stop coming here. I wish they would all go away! Pretty soon this place will be overrun with tourists, stupid tourists."

My friend and I told him about our many backpack trips into the canyons. "I really don't think women should be out backpacking," he said. "They would be better off at home." His wife walked in as he said that, and then walked out, slamming the door behind her.

"A strange fellow," I said. "Does he understand the six P's, that what he writes about has become a call to arms for many of his canyon-loving environmentalist followers? As a writer, did he plan for his message to resonate that way? Does he want to be a folk hero, and if so to who?" My friend shrugged, and smiled.

Emma had once told me a story of a quilting bee she organized to finish her Redwork State Flowers quilt. Now I realized it was a great use of the six P's, a way to teach natural history and happiness at the same time! She had stamped each block with the name and official flower of each of the 48 states. Each flower was embroidered onto a white square, bordered with pink fabric framing red flower sashing, with a red triangle in each corner, and the fabric dyed red to match the color of the embroidery thread. In her scrapbook she wrote, "This quilt was started in 1935 and finished quilting March 12, 1938 with a group of friends. Oh boy what a joy!"

Yellowstone was a special place, where I had shared natural history news, common threads, and joys with many students over many field courses. But, it was not *my* special place. Now I began to think that the canyon country was.

THIS BLOCK OF MY LIFE QUILT WILL BE A MAP OF THE GREATER YELLOWSTONE ECOSYSTEM.

Chapter 13

Binding and Basting

"The rind on a citrus is its finishing touch; the bark on a tree is its natural protection; and the down on a peach encases its rich nectars inside. So it is with a quilt: the binding is a quilt's protection against fraying." [18]

Binding is a narrow strip of fabric used to close the edges of a quilt and protect it from fraying. Basting is a way of loosely tacking a quilt's layers together to hold them for final stitching.

THE NEXT SUMMER I CO-LED A GROUP OF NAVAJO STUDENTS from Tuba City Junior High on a two-week Wilderness Challenge 90-mile backpack in one of the wildest parts of the canyon country, to Rainbow Bridge and around

Navajo Mountain. Access to the trailhead where we began our hike was made by driving 58 miles of paved and gravel roads, then a dirt spur off the main road. We began at the crumbling walls of the old Rainbow Lodge, a remote hotel built by S.I. Richardson and his son in 1924, its last owner Senator Barry Goldwater. After a five-hour van journey to the remains of Rainbow Lodge, the students got out to stretch their legs, wandered to the old lodge, and stepped inside its fallen walls. Looking up in unison, they became still as they realized (they told me later) they had unwittingly violated a traditional Navajo rule against going into ruins, historic or prehistoric, that might still be occupied by spirits of the dead. As one, they turned to the south, extending their arms in front of them, and chanted loudly in Navajo for five minutes. They then walked silently from the ruin, began talking in English, and did not speak of what they had done again. We made dinner and camped overnight 100 yards from the lodge.

The next day, with daytime temperatures of 95 plus degrees, we shouldered our 65-pound backpacks. After four days of hiking a steep up and down trail we arrived at Rainbow Bridge—a natural stone bridge on the edge of Lake Powell (Glen Canyon) called *Nonnezoshe* or “rainbow turned to stone” by the Navajo people, my students told me. Since an Anglo named John Wetherill, guided by Navajos Nasja Begay and Jim Mike, first saw it in 1909, this landmark has become an attraction for Lake Powell boaters because of its easy access from the lake. They went on to say that to the Navajo people Rainbow Bridge stories are of a male and a female rainbow person coming together in perfect union, and frozen in time. This rock rainbow is particularly special as it is the only arch that can be viewed from both sides and is home to several other sites of religious significance to the Navajo people, including the union of the feminine Colorado River and the masculine San Juan River. Sacred offerings cannot be placed at the union of the Colorado and San Juan Rivers now, as it is covered by water, which prevents the Navajo from properly conducting ceremonies that protect them from harsh weather and disease. Because of the increasingly large presence of tourists at Rainbow Bridge, the Navajo people are not able to communicate with the spirits around the Bridge during the day, and their ceremonies cannot be conducted at night after the tourists have left because of the decrees of the spirits. Tourists quite often walk under Rainbow Bridge, which is expressly forbidden by Navajo tradition.

When we got there dozens of tourists were already at the bridge. My group walked near but not to the bridge, with heads bowed.

An Anglo tourist complained, "Now Johnny, don't go too close to that thing. It might fall down."

A very large Anglo tourist lady yelled to her husband, "Dear, I can't walk that far, it's 100 degrees. Let's just take pictures of that stupid arch from here and head back to the boat."

After one student in our group got a nosebleed, we attended to him and left, our students shaking their heads and frowning. We quickly hiked six miles on down the trail around Navajo Mountain. As we came to a running stream, and stopped to fill our water bottles, a man who appeared to weigh 300 pounds was sitting by the stream. He had a gigantic backpack with a gun, sheepskin coat, and fishing pole strapped to its outside. One now empty quart canteen was on a strap around his neck, and his face was as red as a claret cup cactus. I was immediately struck by his seeming lack of understanding of the six P's.

"Where are you going?" my co-leader asked politely.

"I am going to hike along the sandy beaches of Lake Powell and up the San Juan arm of the lake to Mexican Hat," he replied with pride, while wiping his face with a sweat-soaked bandana.

Incredulous, I asked, "Did you know that Lake Powell has no sandy beaches? It was once Glen Canyon, a part of the Colorado River, with steep, sheer walls for much of the shoreline. And besides, that's almost an 80-mile hike at over 100 degrees!"

"Well, there is a sandy beach at Page," he stated flatly.

"I looked at the map there and memorized the entire route, so I don't need a map. I'll just follow the shoreline."

"What will you do for food?" I asked.

"I thought I would fish and hunt," he said.

"And what will you do for water?

"I have a quart canteen that I will fill from the lake when I need to," he said.

"Well most of the time you will not be able to get to the lake to either drink or fish, as there is no shoreline, just sheer canyon walls," I explained as nicely as I could, holding out our map.

"Oh, I thought this line was the trail," he said, pointing to the straight pink line on our map (he had none) that marked the administrative boundary of the Glen Canyon Recreation Area.

"No, this is the trail." I pointed to a squiggly black line that wound in and out of canyons and up and down hills and valleys sometimes four to six miles from the lake shore before swerving off toward the town of Navajo Mountain. He did not reply.

"Good luck," we shrugged, "because you can't always get to the lake cross-country; there are lots of canyons and cliffs in between with no water. Best to go home and do a little more preparation before you do something like this!"

As we headed along the trail toward our campsite we leapfrogged with the lone hiker for six miles. Each time we met, he borrowed water from us, as his canteen was empty. During a break with our group late in the day, we saw him hiking toward us, red-faced and dripping with sweat. Without a word, he walked up to my co-leader, grabbed his water bottle and put its mouth to his mouth, spilling half of the water down his chest.

My co-leader exclaimed, "Man, you are going to die out here! You are nuts!"

The hiker handed the water bottle back and replied, "It's too hot. I'm going to walk to the lake and cool off."

Without another word, he headed out across the slickrock toward the small piece of blue lake we could see far in the distance. We shook our heads, continued on the trail, and arrived at camp near a small stream just off the trail, as we had planned. We asked the group to make dinner, while we went to look for the hiker.

After walking down canyon a couple of miles, we saw him jumping down ledges to get to the stream right next to us. His pack was gone. He dropped into our canyon and ran up to my co-leader, grabbed his water bottle again, and drank without stopping, pouring as much water *on* as *in* his body.

My co-leader said, "You are going to die, buddy. Go home!"

The hiker didn't reply, just kept drinking, then ran over and jumped in the stream fully clothed. After he had cooled off, my co-leader said again, "You are going to die, buddy. Come join us for dinner. Then get back on the trail in the morning and go home!"

He didn't reply, so we shrugged and headed back to camp, but he never came, and we never saw him again.

That night we sat around the campfire and discussed the lone hiker—his lack of preparation, knowledge, skills, and about giving serious thought to life choices. I suggested that any choice made was an investment, has a cost, and the cost is not chump change. We talked about how a coalition of Native and non-Native environmental groups were calling for Lake Powell to be drained, returning the water to its natural level, uncovering sacred sites currently beneath and near the water. Several students nodded in agreement with this idea and said they had friends and family who were members of that coalition.

We had taught the students, but the students taught us as well, that contrasting place-based cultural beliefs create radically different experiences and can prevent or create a true understanding of place. The canyons were quickly becoming my binding of place, one of the ingredients that made me resilient and happy, and sharing them with others helped me develop a strong personal narrative to keep my life from fraying.

THIS BLOCK OF MY QUILT IS A MAP OF CANYON COUNTRY AND A LARGE WATER BOTTLE WITH DROPS OF WATER SPILLING OUT.

Chapter 14

Sashing

"One who works in the earth gathers seed packets and little sprouts, tills the earth, sows her seed, and waits for the flowers to grow. One who works in fabric gathers her pattern, cuts her piece, and carefully sews each petal in place." [19]

Sashing are strips of fabric used to join quilt blocks together carefully and creatively.

THE LANDSCAPES OF MY CHILDHOOD FARM IN THE OZARKS, Arizona and Oregon college classes outdoors, and the wilds of Alaska, Yellowstone and Utah, had created in me a yearning for a rural life, and a need to choose a "place" I felt completely at home, that joined my life experiences together. So, one winter I sought out real estate agents to take me to look at various properties in southeast Utah with the potential of being a NOLS branch school. Most of the land they showed me was raw with no buildings, only chained and burned trees. This was a local method to clear farmland using a 50-foot iron chain strung tight between two tractors, that rips down everything in its path. When I saw the first parcels of chained land, I cringed and frowned. Another day an agent took me to see more chained land, and on the way we drove through an old homestead on the highest point around. A U.S. Geological Survey benchmark near a cabin on the property declared the elevation to be 6,608 feet. We could see mountain ranges and high points in four states: the Bears Ears on Elk Ridge, Abajo and La Sal Mountains in Utah, Lone Cone, San Juan, La Plata Mountains in Colorado, Shiprock in New Mexico, and the Carrizo and Lukachukai Mountains in Arizona. This property was an old homestead, with three old log cabins and four frame buildings built in the 1920s surrounded by piñon and juniper trees and sagebrush, a round grain silo, a log pig shed, chicken coops, and two small horse corrals. Most of the buildings were outbuildings for farm use, but one log cabin looked habitable. There was a hand-dug well 45 feet deep lined with rock, a phone line, electricity, a few fruit trees, and a gravel road. A septic tank, sidewalks, and a cistern were all that remained of the homesteader's house destroyed by fire in the 1960s. These buildings sat on 12 ½ acres surrounded by 200 acres of farm fields and two canyons in the distance. Not a single house was visible from this hilltop, just dryland pinto bean fields, trees, mountains, and blue sky.

"I want to buy that old homestead," I said firmly to the realtor.

"Mormons usually don't sell their homesteads," he replied, "but we can ask."

We went to visit the owner, a long-time farmer himself, and the son of the Mormon farmer who homesteaded the land. When I told him I wanted to buy his old homestead and start an outdoor school, he laughed like a loud foghorn, and said sure he would sell, but needed time to consider the price. The realtor said, "Well I'm not too surprised. That farmer's kids don't want to live there, and he has never met a person he didn't like. He's just that way."

When I called the owner two weeks later from my job in Alaska, he laughed loudly again and said, "My wife and I love your idea of an outdoor school on our old homestead, so how about $12,500?" I smiled and said to mail me the contract and I would sign. The price and view were perfect.

My new home was an island of trees surrounded by a

sea of pinto bean fields. It was 19.5 miles from the nearest town, one mile from the nearest full-time neighbor. It was at the end of a dead-end road. Deer, coyotes, bears, and mountain lions passed by my log cabin windows, and the mood of the Abajo Mountains 15 miles west changed hourly, as white and gray storm clouds gathered around them. I could not see red rocks, but I felt them surrounding me just below these highlands.

The former owners were a family of seven who had lived there from the 1920s to the 1960s. They had hauled their drinking water in a barrel on a horse-drawn wagon each week from a canyon half a mile away. The root cellar they dug was once an Ancestral Puebloan burial ground. They had pulled ancient bones from the dirt walls and reburied them—so the spirits could go back to rest, they said. I heard sounds after dark soon after I moved there. At least one spirit remained in transit, it seemed, hammering and sawing or perhaps pounding and grinding corn on a large stone slab (metate) with a handheld stone (mano). A water dowser friend later envisioned the ghost as a woman who once lived on this homestead, was raised by the Mormon family, but did not want to live as a Mormon. The dowser said the ghost died in her 20s or 30s in the 1920s or 1930s. Her spirit could not rest, I was told, because she felt unwelcome by her Mormon ancestors in the afterlife.

When I moved into the one habitable log cabin after my last summer in Alaska, I brought with me some sourdough starter. I had made the yeast starter by leaving flour and water in a warm place for several days and capturing "wild yeast" cells—tiny microorganisms that exist all around us in soil, on plants, and in the air. My wild yeast starter could raise two loaves of bread to double their original size in one hour. I did not have a refrigerator in my new one-room cabin home. So, I kept the yeast in a jar near the floor, the coolest place when the wood stove was going. After I had gone to bed one night, I heard a hissing noise. Turning on the light, I walked to the corner where the noise seemed to come from and saw the starter jar. I unscrewed the lid slightly, and it blew off in my hands, with the starter climbing from the jar, all over my hand, and onto the floor. It wanted a new life, as did I.

That summer I read *Beyond the Hundredth Meridian*, Wallace Stegner's book about John Wesley Powell's exploration of the Colorado Plateau in 1869, which brought back memories of my high school physiography class with Mr. Poos. I was now living in the landscape Powell had written about. I settled quickly into my homestead, knowing intuitively this was the home "place" for me.

I had lived in another log cabin right below Thumb Butte in college, where I contemplated finding my "place." Emma, a watercolor painter as well as a quilter, once did a miniature close-up painting of Thumb Butte, an isolated square monolith on the edge of Prescott, bordered in a sea of low, dark gray clouds. She walked there often in her red dress and hat, to collect pinecones and rocks for her window displays and as models for her watercolors about Prescott's natural environment, and to contemplate God's hand in shaping her life. Both Emma and I found our "place" when we found sashing that joined our lives with a particular landscape and its people.

THIS BLOCK OF MY QUILT WILL BE THUMB BUTTE AND A LOG CABIN.

Chapter 15

Grain Line

"Whether created for warmth, decorative embellishment, political propaganda, or as a reason for social interaction, quilts and the people who create them are as widespread as they are diverse." [20]

If you cut pattern pieces on the straight of the fabric's grain line … they fall naturally in line with one another and will not buckle when stitched together.

HUMOR IS VERY DIVERSE, AND LIKE A GRAIN LINE, HELPS things fall naturally in line and helps a life promote its own happy continuation. So when the house of the former owners of my new homestead burned to the ground, they rebuilt a new home about four miles away, but left me many treasures in their old buildings: letters, dolls, books, toys, rusted ice-skate blades, a Captain Marvel gun, thick glass bottles, traps, wooden barrels, branding irons, wooden gunstocks, a dinner bell, and a two-foot-long 30-pound iron tractor wrench. They also had left prehistoric artifacts—pottery shards, arrowheads, manos, and metates scattered everywhere.

The chicken shed had been uninhabited for ten years, its roof almost collapsed; the cistern lid was likewise cracked. Mice had nested in their letters, books, dolls, and toys. That winter it was wet; piñon nuts were thick, and the mouse crop good. Lots of mice meant lots of snake food. Almost anytime I walked outside, a rattlesnake was sunning itself, napping, or just cruising for a meal. I devised a plan with friends to move the snakes off. First step was loading an entire two-ton grain truck, loaned to me by the former owners, and removing the mouse habitat from all the buildings to the dump. Second step was to kill six snakes; eat two, turn two into snakeskin hatbands, and hang the last two in a tree. Feeling guilty for killing the snakes, I planned step three—a rattlesnake roundup for any more snakes I found. I invented a roundup stick—a long broom handle with an eyebolt screwed into the end, a stiff rope laid along the stick's length, ending in a small loop through the eyebolt, the rest of the rope held at the top. Each snake I saw, I could slip the loop over its head, pull it tight enough at the neck to hold the snake firmly without harming it, lift the stick in the air with the snake dangling and thrashing, get in my car, hang the stick out the window with my left hand, and drive down the road with my right hand. I then released them in a pile of rocks.

I knew that to fear rattlesnakes was somewhat unfounded; they rarely bite unless cornered or hurt. They do not see well, but can feel the vibrations of lizards and small rodents as they hunt. They rarely travel more than a mile from their den, hunting at night and staying out of sight during long digestive periods. They swallow their babies and often are killed with their young still inside. They cannot strike from a long distance or chase people. In fact, they are wary of people, because we are so much larger. In fact, most wild animals are scared of humans, yet humans fear them enough to have rendered numerous species extinct. "Wild" does not mean out of control. It means "in its natural state." Wild animals are very much in their natural state. Humans want to control them, but if they can't, who is in control? Some say it is one of the various supernatural, immortal beings having special powers over people and nature, but I agree with biologist Joseph Morales who says, "*Life is a system that tends to respond to changes in the environment, and inside itself, in such a way as to promote its own continuation.*" What could be more in control than that?

So when I heard a couple bought the land adjacent to mine just before Christmas that year, I was anxious to get home and see how I might respond to this change in my local environment. Up until now I had no neighbors, and I hoped I would like them. I could not see their trailer from my cabin, which was good as I liked my unobstructed view and privacy. I got home late that mid-January day from visiting family in the Midwest. It was 20 degrees below zero with two feet of snow on the ground. I was just lighting my wood stove, the cabin still cold, when my new neighbors and their two children appeared on my porch. They offered, without my asking, that they had met when the wife ran away from her first husband, who smoked too much pot. She was driving cross country with her tent and kids to escape him, but was too scared to camp. Almost falling asleep at the wheel, she came close to running a semi-truck off the road. The truck driver signaled for her to stop and he yelled at her; she cried and explained her fears, so he offered to follow her until he was to exit the highway, then radioed to a trucker buddy to continue the escort. When he ran out of trucker buddies, the next escort he could suggest was a truck driver hitchhiking to California. She gave him a lift, and he became her new husband a couple months later, and now they were my new neighbors.

When they moved to the edge of the canyon below me, their first idea was to build a resort at the highway turnoff north of me, and second to grow potatoes in the canyon below by the spring. They planned to move into their single-wide trailer that fall, but the first heavy snow had collapsed the roof right after they set it up. For the moment, they were living in a rented house in town. They fixed the roof in the spring, moved into the trailer, and the husband hooked up propane gas lines for their cooking stove. He mistook a water line for the gas line and left one side of a T-fitting open. When he turned the gas on and lit the stove, it blew up in his face. His wife brought him to my house for first aid, and after I administered some, she took him to the hospital. The family moved back into town so he could heal from the first- and second-degree burns on his face and arms.

The husband was an upholsterer by trade who worked in vinyl. After he recovered, he and his family returned to the trailer. Another neighbor gave the family 20 chickens and three goats as housewarming gifts. My neighbors decided to build a chicken coop. He framed it with wood and finished it by wrapping the framing with red vinyl for walls. He didn't include a roof or doors, so the chickens could not get into their new home and could fly out the top if placed inside. He told me the chickens and goats could forage for food and water and live under their trailer, so they did not need to feed or house them. The chickens became wild and the goats froze to death later. The wife later told a mutual friend, who gave them the goats and chickens, that when they met me that first winter, I had whipped off my bra because I knew her husband liked women without bras. Really I thought, who are these funny people, and how should I respond to this?

After that family left, the land and single-wide mobile home were purchased by seven gay men from San Francisco. When I went to meet them, I learned they planned to grow pot in the canyon below us in the spring. Late that summer, at harvest time, they went to the local grocery store and bought **all** the Ziploc bags the store carried. The clerk checking them out thought it odd and alerted the sheriff, who staked out their place, found their growing location, and busted them. I watched two of them being hauled off to jail. Really? What were these guys thinking, buying a large quantity of Ziploc bags in rural Utah—but I liked them!

Scientists have categorized nine different types of humor: physical, self-deprecating, surreal, improvisational, wit, topical, observational, bodily, and dark. Diverse humor kept me sane and healthy when some improvisational, observational, and surreal times allowed me to relinquish stifling rules, and helped me grow beyond my boundaries.

THIS BLOCK OF MY LIFE QUILT WILL BE A RED VINYL CHICKEN COOP.

Chapter 16

Lattice Strips

"Quilting knows no boundaries of color, race, or country of origin... But quilting was born of necessity, to keep out the cold. Anything that could be used for quilts was, and any design, was acceptable." [21]

Lattice strips are narrow pieces of fabric that separate and frame quilt blocks, making each block stand out.

DIVERSE FRIENDSHIPS AND EXPERIENCES MAKE A LIFE STAND out. When I suggested to the friend who installed my new hot tub, that he could use it while I was out of town, he readily agreed. As he rounded the last curve in the dark, and was driving the final mile of gravel road to my house, his car's headlights framed and illuminated a deer running past, pursued by a mountain lion in mid-leap. My friend never saw the conclusion—this life and death snapshot merged into the black of night. When he got to my house and was sitting alone in the hot tub, with starlight tacking the darkness, he heard a car drive up. After about 15 minutes, a man walked to the back of the house and a voice came out of the pitch black dark.

"Is this your house?" the man asked.

"No," my friend answered, "but a friend of mine owns it. And who are you?"

"My name is Manfred. I am Navajo and have come to see about some hot water," the stranger said.

They talked for a few minutes and then my friend invited Manfred into the hot tub. Manfred said, "Ok, but just a minute," disappeared, and returned ten minutes later with his wife and grandmother. Manfred undressed, got into the tub, and eventually his wife and grandmother removed their clothes and climbed into the hot tub with the two men. Manfred's grandmother produced a teapot full of peyote tea, shared it with all, then sang a song in Navajo. In Navajo culture a "Way" is a ceremony conducted for healing, blessing, or medicine. It includes a song or prayer chant, may include the use of peyote or other herbs, and is meant to rid a person of a persistent problem or end an episode of witchcraft. Grandma might have been conducting a Hot-Tub-Way that night with her family and my friend.

When I returned, my friend told me this story in a puzzled voice, and asked if I knew Manfred. "No," I replied.

I later told a Navajo friend this story and he said simply, "They were Skinwalkers—Navajo wolves, or witches," then added, "if you see a Skinwalker, something bad will happen to you."

I thought about this and said to him that nothing bad had happened to me. He replied, "But you were not in the hot tub; did something bad happen to your friend?"

I thought for two seconds and said, "Yes. Two years later he committed suicide."

Who were these visitors, how did they find my hot tub that night, how did they know I lived there? Were they still at my house or had they now left? All questions I could not answer.

Three years later, as I sat in my same hot tub with another friend, we watched the Hale-Bopp comet move across the unobstructed night sky. It had a luminous tail, fluoresced by hidden sunlight, gravitationally bound to the sun and made of leftovers: primitive, cosmic debris never incorporated into a solid planet. I wanted to hold a piece of this comet's material in my hand and squeeze it together, but it would only come apart, like a poorly compacted snowball. An owl hooted once, then twice. I looked across the ground and saw a pair of glowing, blinking yellow eyes. I looked up again and saw a blanket of yellow stars, maybe 100 billion, all blinking. There were some familiar patterns—the Big Dipper, Orion, the North Star—a sky full of yellow blinks tying together this universal black quilt and my place in it. I had heard from Navajo friends that owls were bad luck. Ten years later this friend died of breast cancer. So maybe the visitors were still around?

Later my cousin, her boyfriend, their two dogs, and my dog and I took a trip to Kino Bay in Mexico and camped on the beach. One day we met a man named Art who told us he had been an original cartoonist for Disney, but was now retired. He was waiting for his wife to join him, but feared she never would, and may have found another lover. He invited us to accompany him on his boat to Tiburon Island, several miles off the coast of Kino Bay. We loaded our camping gear and three dogs on his deck, and left the next day. That night we built a fire, ate shrimp he had bought from local fishermen, and laid our sleeping bags on the shore. Coyotes howled nearby, just outside the fire's light, and even though it was 85 degrees I shivered. In the early morning, lying on my stomach in my sleeping bag, I lifted my head and saw a skinny, grayish-brown coyote sitting two feet from my face, staring at me. I did not feel afraid, as our dogs snored on. The coyote cocked his head from side to side, lifted his leg and scent marked, as we stared silently at each other for a full two minutes, his nose twitching. He trotted away wagging his tail, and I went back to sleep. I had read that in Seri mythology (natives of the area), Coyote is a buffoon that is easily tricked, or he is the trickster. Yet I did not feel tricked, but perhaps Art had been by his wife who never showed up, or the coyote tricked me into thinking he was real.

I went back to college and told Emma this last story; she told me about some of her male friends and their lack of fear at trying something new, usually done by women. One was an embroidery artist, Arendt Kuelper. She wrote to him after reading an article in the *Denver Post* about his exceptional needlework on a wall hanging of the Last Supper, to compliment him on his fine work. He wrote back, saying that ordinary embroidery thread was not fine enough for him, and it did not come in enough colors. "It won't give a piece of needlework art the proper life ... I just draw the picture with the thread, sort of sketching with the needle as I go along," Kuelper wrote. Later he wrote, "Call what you and I are doing a hobby, strange as it may seem, neither you or I could do it if it were not inside of us ... it is something finer than what we can see or feel."

Emma also told me about Leopold Aul, a professional musician who learned to quilt from his father at age 14. To achieve his intricate designs, he cut small, precise pieces, basted them into a foundation, and delicately cross-stitched all the edges using a fine buttonhole twist stitch.

She told me about Milan Johnson, a professional furniture maker who taught cabinet work at a high school in New Hampshire. He started out making intricate inlaid boxes; one incorporated 31,000 pieces of colored wood. Later his work evolved into quilting, and he used the same love for detailed design by employing stencils to shape his fabric squares, finishing them with 190,000 quilt stitches. Emma told me one day, "Mr. Milan Johnson, of Keene, New Hampshire is 85 and does the most perfect piecing and quilting himself. No woman could beat his work."

What Emma and I learned from diverse individual human and nonhuman friendships—a lack of fear, and trying something new—framed our lives in many ways, especially when experiences were place-based.

THIS BLOCK OF MY QUILT WILL BE THE BIG DIPPER, A COYOTE, DEER AND MOUNTAIN LION.

Chapter 17

Negative Space

"I want a voice in the world, and my quilts give me that voice ... My quilts encourage people to slow down and to think about our daily lives—what we are doing to ourselves and to our environment." [22]

Negative (background or white) space gives definition and depth to the whole quilt project by adding contrast and allows the main design to shine. Large segments of negative space can add weight and focus to the design area of the piece, drawing you in and allowing the positive space (the object in the quilt or design space) to be the focus.

UNDERSTANDING THE IMPORTANCE OF PERSEVERANCE, HARD work, and how our impact on the environment defines our future, helped me understand that empathy and occasional tolerance for contrasting views allowed my life design to shine and gave it depth.

I explored negative political space by protesting the Vietnam War in high school. In college I started exploring background green space when I took a college class on Wilderness. I continued exploring green spaces while canoeing the Eleven Point River in Arkansas in the 1970s with my father and a friend. It is one of the prettiest and most peaceful rivers in the Ozarks, and had just been designated a "Wild and Scenic" river by Congress. At the put-in, locals kicked up gravel at us with their trucks and yelled obscenities, so we quickly got in our canoes and pushed off. On day three of our trip, we rounded a bend in the river and entered a small rapid. Just as we gathered speed, we spotted two strands of barbed wire strung across the river, one at neck level, one at canoe level, and a man running away into the bushes. The first wire turned out to be loose enough to push up and go under, the other loose enough to push down and go over, as he hadn't finished tightening them. Shaking, we pulled immediately to shore, my friend and I took the barbed wire down, while my father hid in the bushes near the canoes. After a few minutes, the man came out of the bushes toward our canoes with his hands out, bending over to push them into the river. My father stepped quickly out of the bushes and asked the man what he wanted. He spun around, said he was looking for some wild boars, and ran. We got into our canoes with the rolled-up wire and continued down the river. That night around the campfire we talked about if this man was blaming us for this public land designation and why he was so angry that he would want to injure or strand us. I was learning that anger leads to fear, fear to hate of the "other," and hate to the dark side. Yet I might have some empathy for him and those at the put-in if I could understand their point of view—just not their way of expressing it.

I encountered the same sense of displaced anger after moving to Utah full time to work as a wilderness specialist for the Bureau of Land Management in 1979. Fifteen years had passed since Congress passed the Wilderness Act in 1964, with a goal to identify and designate wilderness-quality lands on all National Park Service and Forest Service lands, and federally protect them. These were places where "man is a visitor and does not remain." The Federal Land Policy and Management Act (FLPMA) was then passed in 1976, issuing guiding legislation for identifying and designating wilderness lands on Bureau of Land Management lands. In 1977 and 1978, a half-million acres of BLM land in San Juan County, Utah had been identified through an initial cursory inventory as having wilderness characteristics. Two co-workers and I were hired for six months to conduct the intensive inventory for over half a million acres of possible wilderness-quality lands in San Juan County, with FLPMA as our Bible on how to do our job. It defined a road, solitude, naturalness, and more. Our job was to check each initial inventory unit's boundaries, make sure they met the legal criteria for Wilderness designation. If they did, BLM would be obligated to manage each unit as a Wilderness Study Area until Congress finally passed a bill making it an official Wilderness. According to FLPMA wilderness guidelines, we were to decide if all the units in the initial inventory had these qualities:

1. Outstanding opportunities for solitude;
2. Outstanding opportunities for primitive and unconfined recreation;
3. Were substantially natural;
4. Were more than 5,000 acres in size; and
5. Had man-made intrusions within their boundaries that could be removed in five years.

After I began, I asked my immediate supervisor's boss how I should conduct the inventories and how the state BLM office wanted us to be consistent with FLPMA and national standards.

"Oh, just make it up as you go along," she said.

"How could this be right?" I asked. She just shrugged and told me if we ever went on an inventory trip together, she would never go in the field if there were no toilets close by. Her boss would never go out at all, as the bouncing on four-wheel drive roads made his hemorrhoids hurt.

So my co-worker and I decided, with our immediate supervisor's approval, that we had to hike, fly in a helicopter, ride horseback, or drive around each of the initial inventory units thoroughly. How else could we make an appropriate decision about its Wilderness qualities?

One area we intensively inventoried was the 109,000-acre Mancos Mesa unit, one of the largest initial inventory units BLM had. It had been proposed in 1976 to be an "Instant Study Area," which meant it so obviously had the above wilderness characteristics that it should receive instant designation by BLM with no further study. Grand Gulch and Dark Canyon were made Instant Study Areas in 1976, while Mancos Mesa was not. No one would tell me why. My co-worker and I drove the borders of Mancos Mesa in a truck, trying to determine what disqualified it for instant wilderness protection. It featured wide expanses of slickrock and sagebrush, blackbrush, and sand dunes. The distant Henry Mountains were the predominant view from anywhere we looked. The mesa was sliced into at least eight canyons that dropped sharply off on one side into Glen Canyon Recreation Area managed by the National Park Service, now Lake Powell. A few old mining exploration roads penetrated its interior, but a sand slide had made them impassable. These roads had been built after the passage of FLPMA, making them technically illegal, but they had not been reclaimed by the BLM, despite federal direction to do so. It looked like perfect Wilderness land to us. We noted that a local county commissioner had an inactive uranium mine on its east side. We asked if we could explore the rest of the area's interior on foot, but our big boss told us it was "too big and remote."

So, a few weeks later, he hired a helicopter to drop my co-workers and me on the ground to take pictures in three different spots multiple times. After the first drop the helicopter pilot picked me up, but not finding my co-workers, went to refuel, eat lunch, and look again. This took half of the day we had left. Meanwhile my co-workers were zipped up inside their flight suits to avoid the gnats that were eating their ears and faces. We only had time for one more drop that day that concluded in one hour. When we asked to go back and finish the inventory on another day, we were told there was not enough time. My co-worker and I determined this area met the qualifications for Wilderness, based on what we had seen, and recommended it in our report.

I later learned that my supervisor's boss, the woman in charge of the wilderness inventory in the BLM's District office, the one who wouldn't go anywhere outside too far from a toilet, was married to the manager of a large mining corporation that had claims in some of BLM's proposed initial inventory wilderness lands. Her boss, the one with hemorrhoids, was a Forest Service lifer who hated the desert, as it had few trees, yet he had been hired to study it for wilderness qualities. I told my immediate boss these two people had a conflict of interest. I was told to work on maps in the office and stay out of the field. I learned the next day that this part of Utah was in huge demand by energy companies for oil exploration drilling, and others wanted it for mining, logging, and off-road vehicle use. Again, I saw a conflict of direction and purpose but my higher ups had no authority to fire or replace them.

The next week, I was part of the BLM staff team conducting a community meeting to inform the public of our progress on the intensive wilderness inventory. A county commissioner shouted that we were taking all the income-producing lands away from the county and warned, "All you guys better start traveling in twos and threes, because we're going to get you!"

"Is that a threat, sir?" my immediate boss asked, to which the commissioner responded, "No sir, that's a promise." Our state senator quickly grabbed the county commissioner by his arm and escorted him from the room. The commissioner continued his threats in a radio interview the next day. "If you see any BLM people broken down by the side of the road, don't stop to pick them up!" he fumed in the interview.

All BLM employees who attended the public meeting were asked to write a report. I happened to turn mine in first, which somehow was then sent to Congress. The county commissioner eventually came by the BLM office and apologized to me for his inappropriate comments at the public meeting. I accepted his apology, but I still took his threats and encouragement of bullying of BLM employees seriously. After my seasonal job ended, I saw that Mancos Mesa had not been recommended for wilderness designation, based on its "lack of solitude." Arch Canyon, also recommended by us, was excluded due to its small size even though it was adjacent to an already declared Forest Service Wilderness Area; so, if combined with the BLM parcel, it would qualify for the 5,000-acre-plus criterion. Two other units we found to qualify as wilderness were not recommended to the state BLM by our district office.

My job was over, yet I continued to explore this

negative space by joining a lawsuit, writing long letters about my unprofessional experiences with the BLM intensive wilderness inventory staff and policies, testifying before Congress, and being interviewed by national TV networks. At a later public hearing on BLM's proposed wilderness areas, Utah's then U.S. Congressman Wayne Owens attempted to explain why he had introduced a federal bill to declare 5.7 million acres of BLM land as Wilderness. Several people spoke in angry protest, asking how the congressman could do this, warning that it would ruin local livelihoods, and force children to leave town for jobs. I thanked the congress-man for his foresight and courage.

A local rancher rose and said, "I was out near White Canyon the other day, and I came upon that bunch, that girl over there and her bunch, they smelled so bad they nearly scared my horse out from under me! And the toilet paper—why, they throw their toilet paper here; they throw their toilet paper there—why, if that's the kind of people we're going to have in wilderness, I don't want any!" The audience clapped loudly; the congressman quizzically asked me if this guy was for real, I shook my head affirmatively, and we both laughed.

That lawsuit was won; many acres were restored as BLM wilderness study areas, including Mancos Mesa and Arch Canyon. (Eventually the intensive inventory was completely redone by BLM and citizen groups, which recommended 5.9 million acres of Wilderness quality land, of which to this day only a tiny portion has been designated by Congress, but has resulted in continued protection for these lands from much development.)

Emma had told me many stories of male quilting friends whose work influenced the negative and positive space in her quilting. One was Dad Pratt, born in Manchester, England in 1851 and then emigrated to Philadelphia in 1886. He became fascinated with the artistic possibilities of the patchwork quilt through his carpet-making skills. He would piece together thousands of small silk squares into unusual mosaic patterns. He told Emma it took him 50 years to win more than 400 ribbons from each state through perseverance and love of hard work.

She told me of Harry Kendig, a railroad car repairman from Pennsylvania who learned the needle arts from his mother. He wrote Emma, "I started quilting when I was 14 and am now 65, so you see how much influence my mother had on my life." He sent Emma pictures of his quilts—Grandmother's Flower Garden, Wild Rose, Morning Glory, Yellow Dahlia, and Irish Chain—each with more than 5,000 pieces of fabric sewn together. She made a window display of his quilt pictures and letters.

Harry told Emma if anyone else made a stitch in one of his quilts, he had to take it out and stitch it himself, perfect work was so important to him.

Another, Albert Small, was from England, but later lived in Illinois where he worked with machinery and dynamite at a sand plant. As a relief from the dangers of his job, he took up quilting. After watching his wife and daughter quilt, he wagered with them that he could make a quilt with more and smaller patches than they could. He wrote to Emma that he put his quilts together in the evenings, as he loved the peace quilting brought him. His final mosaic quilt with 124,000 pieces landed a mention on Paul Harvey's *Strange as It Seems* radio broadcast.

Our negative life experiences allowed the positive life experiences to be our focus, gave us depth, and added interest. They encouraged us to slow down and think about our daily lives—what we were doing to ourselves and to our environment.

THIS BLOCK OF MY QUILT WILL BE A HELICOPTER, A CANOE, AND A LETTER.

Chapter 18

Pins

"Quiltmakers ... look backward and forward at the same time. Our quilts become an avenue to self-expression and a chance to communicate to future viewers, as well as a link with those homey values we fear our society is losing: warmth, family, sharing." [23]

Pins are used to hold fabrics together, so patterns match, before stitching together. Re-inserting pins makes corrections in a quilt design, an inevitable part of the quilt making process.

IN LIFE, CHANGE IS INEVITABLE, SO TO BE HAPPY ONE MUST love it, embrace it, and manage it. Since change to your home "place" inevitably happens, why do some resist change so much?

With that in mind, some years later while leading a Prescott College freshman orientation group on a two-week backpack trip from the Aquarius Plateau, down through Capitol Reef's Waterpocket Fold, up over the 11,500-foot Mount Ellen, and back down to the Burr Desert, we came upon a two-holer outhouse at 10,000 feet in the Henry Mountains—100 miles due west of my desert home. I assumed it was built by a prospector, with its walls and seats of old barn wood, but no door. Wide slits between the boards allowed the breeze to blow in and up for a fast dry. While lingering there for 20 minutes I held a map on my lap identifying with my finger what I could see to the north and east—the Aquarius Plateau, Capitol Reef, the Abajo mountains, La Sal mountains, and the Burr Desert at a distance of more than 200 miles. About 30 miles away was a town of 200 souls called Hanksville.

After identifying all these specific locations of my larger home place, I was inspired to build my own outhouse at my desert home, a one-holer made of the same logs as my house, with a door I always left propped open. It had solid walls, but the breeze could still blow up, refreshingly cold on a winter day. With the door open I could see the Abajo Mountains up close, Horsehead Canyon, and the Bears Ears. During visits to the outhouse, I usually wrote in my journal as a way to wake up, think, plan and create. I wrote about how we "civilized" folks have become disconnected from the land and the things that keep us alive and healthy, how we have forgotten where everyday things come from and where they go. We had come to expect that chicken just comes in plastic wrap from the grocery store and water from a tap. We do not think of how we get oil to make plastic or the process to convert it. We do not think of the farmer who plants the grain for the chicken, the quantity of rainfall to make the grain grow, or chickens falling prey to disease or predation. We do not think of the rivers, rain, snowfall, pipes, mountains, gravity, collection points, glue, faucets, pumps, or sewage plants needed to produce clean tap water.

To me the flush toilet is a symbol of this disconnection. In the past people dug individual holes for their waste. They buried or concentrated waste so the earth could recycle it into food. Later it was a ritual, an essential part of community and living, to dig a large hole for the whole village. It often took days of backbreaking work. Once larger communities developed and came together, they invented screening devices for privacy, then invented open sewers running down the middle of community streets. Their waste was obvious then. With "civilization" came a need to hide our waste, our connection to the earth. Dirty = bad = unhealthy. Then Thomas Crapper invented the flush toilet. Waste was out of sight, out of mind. Sanitize, forget, disconnect. Flush it away so someone else can deal with it, which improved public health, but not public understanding of essential life processes.

So when my mother came to visit, and I still had no flush toilet, I decided to order a portable toilet from Montgomery Ward as I knew she disliked outhouses. I left an hour early to pick up the toilet in the town she was flying into and headed to the airport. As I watched her exit the small commuter plane, she was struggling with her purse and carrying a large garbage bag. When she came through the gate door, I hugged her as she said, "I knew you only had an outhouse, so I brought my own Porta-Potty. That way I won't have to go outside in the cold and at night."

I burst out laughing and said, "I bought you a Porta Potty today too, and it's in the car." We both had to sit down to catch our breath while laughing. During her visit, I used the outhouse, and she used **both** portable toilets.

While sitting in the outhouse one day during Mom's visit I wrote in my journal about how Emma's museum started with quilts, dolls, and thimbles and evolved to scrapbooks, window displays, and paintings—inspired by landscapes and made by people around her. One of her favorite quilts was a Grandmother's Flower Garden baby quilt she had made in a honeycomb pattern that would fit perfectly over the door of my outhouse to keep the breeze out on a cold winter day.

"It's just random pieces of material, but look what they can do to give joy," I remembered Emma had told me in years past, and smiled.

Many random moments were being sewn together to create my life quilt design fertilized by humor. My morning moments connected me with the earth and homey values I feared society was losing: warmth, family, sharing, in a room with a view. As I eliminated my waste, I did not waste my elimination.

Another random moment pinned into my life design was during that summer when I was a Forest Service wildland fire crew chief. I had heard rumors that one of my team, the son of a local sheriff, had been abused as a child. One morning he arrived at our work yard while all the seasonal employees were preparing. He got out of his car, opened the trunk, took a rattlesnake in each hand, and began twirling them over his head, running toward the youngest female firefighter yelling, "Want to pet my snake?" As she ran from him, I chased him, and demanded he free the snakes. He did so, while glaring at me, growling and grinding his teeth. Later that same day I found him in the Forest Service shop wrapping a stick with barbed wire, pounding nails in its top. When I asked what he was doing, he said he was making a stick to beat up Navajo people. I ordered him to stop, immediately called my boss, and said he needed to be dismissed. He wasn't fired right then, and I never got an explanation, but a few days later he was fired for building a dysfunctional fence and being found sleeping on the job in the closet where the Forest Service stored sleeping bags.

Some days after that, I was monitoring a fire call on the radio made to the District Ranger by a seasonal employee up on the mountain. He was reporting five smoke plumes from fires on Elk Ridge near Bears Ears. Then there was a shuffle-drop-scuttle noise, and then a voice I recognized saying, "Let it burn, there's nothing down there. Let it burn."

"Who is this?" the District Ranger replied.

"It's me, your permit holder. Just let it burn. There's nothing down there." I recognized the voice and attitude. It was the guy who had accused me of throwing toilet paper here and there at the public hearing some years back.

"Well how do you know there's nothing down there?" the District Ranger asked.

"I just know, and the range needs some thinning so more grass can grow, so let it burn!"

"We can't do that sir. It's been Forest Service policy for 80 years to put out all fires. We are sending out a crew." After more scuffling noise, the seasonal employee came back on the radio to give more details of each fire's location. "Ten four," I replied, "See ya soon."

My crew and I took an hour to reach Elk Ridge. Enroute, we passed a speeding truck with four people in it—the permit holder, his father, his uncle, and a cousin. I recognized all of them, I had bought my land from one of them. They didn't wave to us in our green Forest Service truck, just rushed by. We arrived at a corral full of horses, parked, and hiked down with water-filled backpacks to the first fire—a quarter-acre blaze. As we worked on putting it out I noticed horse tracks and matches all around the blaze. At each of five fires we found the same thing—horse tracks and matches around the blazing trees. We put them all out and the next day, I told the District Ranger what we had found and asked him to discipline the permit holder. He shook his head, but never did anything to the permit holder or his cohorts that I knew of.

I was becoming increasingly frustrated with the District Ranger. One day he told me he was planning a destructive treatment near Bears Ears, like chaining or logging. I told him that was unwise as this area was sacred to Native people and he would have to take that into account legally before treatments could happen, if at all. He said the area was not sacred, I said I had read and heard it was. We argued back and forth for an hour, and finally I said, "Well I will do the research and prove it to you." A friend and I spent two months compiling 90 pages of letters, articles, books, excerpts, and interviews with Navajo and Hopi people called, "The Bears Ears Report: Documentation of a Sacred Place." I gave him the report, and no treatments occurred then, but I had no idea how prescient this concept would be in years to come. Thirty years later a 1.34 million-acre Bears Ears National Monument was created by President Obama based on the hard work of several native and non-native environmental groups, shortly thereafter shrunk by two-thirds by the next president, and then four years later restored to 1.36 million acres by President Biden and his Secretary of Interior Deb Haaland, a member of Laguna Pueblo, again with the hard work of several Native and non-Native environmental groups.

Two weeks later I was assigned to assist the county weed sprayer for a couple weeks. I drove; he sprayed. One day I asked him what chemicals we were spraying on the invasive thistles in the forest, as I was concerned that they were toxic to me and to him. Certainly some of my Forest Service experiences had been toxic.

"Well, you know what they sprayed out of the showerheads on the Jews in World War II? That's what we are spraying on the thistles," he responded quickly.

I looked at him horrified and said, "As someone who was raised Jewish I need to ask, are these Jewish weeds?" He laughed, but I frowned and the next day asked my supervisor to take me off this detail after explaining why. He did.

A few years later a pickup truck pulled up in my driveway, and out stepped a man with a cowboy hat and bowlegged gait. I recognized him as my accuser from the public hearing, the guy who started the forest fires, also a widower. He removed his hat and shook hands with me and my parents who were visiting. Then he looked at me and said, "I want to take you for a walk."

"OK," I replied flatly.

He walked quickly toward the canyon behind my house and blurted out loudly, "Well, you married yet?"

"No," I smiled.

"Why not? You ain't getting any younger," he yelled.

I laughed and said, "Well I just haven't met the right guy yet."

He spun on his heel, marched back toward the house, and said no more. I had to run to keep up, and when we got back to my house he jumped in his truck, slammed the door, and screeched away. I told my parents all about this guy, his (I assumed) marriage proposal, and his anger—especially toward me and the congressman a few years back, who believed that public lands belonged to all Americans, not just locals. My parents and I laughed while pondering why this guy would propose marriage if he was so angry with me?

Two nights later my parents and I went to dinner with a 60-year-old local mechanic friend who did not have a cowboy hat, but was a true character, someone I had something in common with. He had been born in Texas and moved to Utah when his Dad saw an ad for free homestead land. He claimed that his good health came from years of consuming three cloves of garlic a day, hot jalapeños, and good scotch. He and I had become friends while he was repairing my orange 1956 Willys Jeep with a Pabst Blue Ribbon beer sticker on the front door. Our friendship was further cemented when I walked into his shop one day and replaced all his pinup pictures of naked women with pinups of naked men.

"Society is in transition," I said. He just laughed and laughed. The naked men pictures were gone the next time I stopped by, and the naked women were back. At dinner with my parents, he turned to my mother and said, "That daughter of yours sure is a cute little shit!" She dropped her fork, laughing.

Later I met a cowboy who told me stories of his work

with an environmental group to help protect wild lands in Wyoming and his work with cows on the ranch where he lived. Very different from many of the cowboys I had met here. He told me of the cowboy stories he had published. A seeker of common ground I thought, kind of like me. I picked up his cowboy hat so I could sit on the only chair and talk more with him, setting his hat down on a table on its brim. He picked up a stick, hit his hand with it, and glared at me, "Don't you know how to treat a cowboy's hat?!"

My stomach knotted and I cowered a bit, thinking he might hit me. I looked at him quizzically, laughed cautiously, and asked, "Why did you do that?"

He yelled, "A cowboy's hat is his most important possession. I would think you would know that and treat it with respect. Always set a hat on its top, never on its brim!"

I laughed again and said, "People are more important than hats." He glared at me, eyes red and hard, not laughing. I knew the Western cowboy hat was recognized around the world as part of "cowboy" lore. And I knew that in the early days, it was valued for being functional, with the wide brim protecting cowboys from the sun and rain. It was also used to signal others, fan a campfire, swat a horse or pull water out of a stream. I even knew that John B. Stetson was credited with designing and marketing the first cowboy hat, which he called the "Boss of the Plains." So I told him that maybe a cowboy hat had feelings, and could be insulted, but it was not the boss of me.

When I pin these random but similar moments together into my life design, I know that in building human relationships some elements connect, like mutual love, kindness, and understanding, but others like political beliefs may not. By reinserting and reshaping life events that held me together with mindfulness—the art of slowing and deepening my breathing and allowing thoughts to pass without indulging them—then later re-examining these thoughts and perhaps changing opinions, it ensured my life design worked. I was mindfully learning to reflect on the demands of a world in transition, by loving and truly getting to know individuals—not using a broad brush to hate a group of "others"—and seeking some common ground. This is what had the uncanny ability to speak to me.

Why are some unable to acknowledge global factors that bring about local change, or understand that change is a natural part of life? In resistance they choose to hate change, fear and blame the "other," which only elevates their blood pressure and hardens veins feeding their heart.

THIS BLOCK OF MY QUILT WILL BE BEAR'S EARS, AN OUTHOUSE, AND A COWBOY HAT.

Part Three

PLACE AS THE BINDING OF A LIFE QUILT

"The good wives ... had a habit of saving every scrap ... and constructed of them rainbow shapes ... to bring about ... substantial beauty, warmth, and comfort."

- Harriet Beecher Stowe

Chapter 19

Thimble

"Global thinking promises to be a real challenge for some of us who already have enough difficulty with local thinking ... In such an age quiltmaking has its place. Every stitch taken in a creative spirit is an answer to despair; every knotted thread an affirmation of peaceful human endeavor ... After all, the needle was invented to bind things together." [24]

A thimble is a finger shield that protects from needle pricks during stitching, guides the needle, and prevents slipping.

AN IDEA BEGAN PERCOLATING IN MY MIND TO START A SCHOOL that would eventually grow to build a community of educators to help solve some of the Colorado Plateau's problems—such as high unemployment, poor academic preparation, lack of trained workforce, and teachers' skills—by offering place-based outdoor education programs. Place-based education, I was learning, was a good way to improve engagement of students, renew teachers' skills, and provide jobs for youth, particularly members of nearby Native American communities.

This would be challenging from the one-room log cabin where I lived, so I decided to build a house and restore the cabins on my property to serve as office and basecamp for the school. When they were livable, but not finished, I bought 30 15-minute series topographic maps of the land that stretched about 7,500 square miles around my home. I thumbtacked them to the wall, like wallpaper on a whole wall of my living room, so each contour line, stream, trail, road, and boundary joined correctly to the adjacent map. I drew every hiking route, trail, road, and spring I had personally hiked in the area and laminated them for protection. Using a thimble, I stuck the final tack where my home was located in Township 38 South, Range 25 East, Section 14. I studied them weekly, added new information as I explored a new route, noting where I had to climb up or down a dry waterfall or go around it. In my library were maps of other parts of the Colorado Plateau I had hiked, with routes drawn in, stacked in a neat pile. One day I bought a larger scale map of the entire Plateau, laid it on a table, stood back and realized the ground I had been pacing across for the last 20 years was 130 million square miles shaped like a heart.

As the school grew and I needed a bigger office I took the maps to my new office in town. Friends came from all over to study my wall maps and add their new routes. Over the next years many continued to mark these maps with every hiking trail, spring, off-trail route, impassable pour-off, road, and dirt track they ever walked, found, or were told about. Land management officials from up to 50 miles away would come to study my maps. On the wall next to the maps was a quote from Wallace Stegner's *Beyond the Hundredth Meridian*, about John Wesley Powell and his explorations of the Colorado Plateau:

It is the Plateau Province ... Here geological and human history have at least a poetic similarity ... Though the geologic record in the Plateau Province is probably as clear as it is anywhere on earth, the boundary between ignorance and knowledge, between speculation and certainty, is often no more than ... an enigmatic unconformity.

First the school was called Windsong Wilderness

Expeditions, then Four Corners School of Outdoor Education, now Canyon Country Discovery Center. The initial idea was that people would come to my homestead from all over the world to launch their journey into the redrock country of southern Utah. They would join educational journeys (Southwest Ed-Ventures) called Rock Art and Geology of the San Juan River, Searching for the Northern Boundaries of the Kayenta Anasazi, Writing Down the River, and Archaeological Excavations of Old Man Cave. All were led by authors, experts, and guides who had spent their lives teaching about, researching, and caring for these lands of the Colorado Plateau. Authors like Ann Zwinger (a naturalist) and Page Stegner (Wallace Stegner's son) and rock art specialists like Sally Cole and Polly Schaafsma educated groups. I eventually offered citizen science Ed-Ventures like the excavations of Old Man Cave, Glade Road Rock shelter, and Miller Camp. We also documented rock art and habitation sites in the San Juan Arm of Lake Powell, Kaiparowits Plateau, Slickhorn Canyon, the Ute Tribal Park, Butler Wash, and the Escalante Canyons. We conducted wildlife surveys for the National Park Service, BLM, and the Forest Service for peregrine falcons and bighorn sheep on the San Juan River, Grand Canyon National Park, Dark Canyon Wilderness area, Grand Gulch, Desolation and Gray Canyons of the Green River, much of the San Juan Resource area of BLM, and Ruby, Horsethief, and Westwater Canyons of the Colorado River. We did wolf and polar bear research in Canada and Alaska.

A Southwest Ed-Venture Butler Wash rock art documentation 1996 participant said, "*The expedition more than met my expectations, I was able to contribute to worthwhile research.*" Another said: "*We knew we had done our work and were part of the discovery ... But we would never be quite the same.*"

Later we conducted a cross-cultural exchange program, "Have You Ever Seen a Rainbow at Night"—between an art coach, the Denver Art Museum, three Denver public middle schools, and the community of Montezuma Creek, Utah—that used art as a vehicle to learn about Navajo culture. A participant said, "*Thank you for one of the best experiences of my life. I loved learning about the culture of the Navajo. The beauty of the land was amazing.*"

As programs grew, I would cook meals for participants in my home; my bathroom would be used for showers, and my living room for group gatherings. Participants would spend the first night of their expedition in my log cabin bunkhouse, to get to know one another. I would haul 10,000 gallons of water each month, 1,000 gallons at a time, into my cistern.

From my basecamp they would begin to build a sense of community with others who would share their Ed-Venture, while pushing themselves physically and mentally. They would see things they otherwise might never see—rugged scenery, ancient Indian artifacts, and a night sky full of brilliant stars. When they returned from their trip, they would be happy, rested, more knowledgeable, and excited. Their final night would include stories of the trip, exchanging addresses with newfound friends, and saying goodbye to their small, intentional community, again in my living room. They would fall in love with the place and experience. Many would return to the Plateau again and again.

Starting the school made me a target of local rumors from those who suspected I had environmentalist motives. The sheriff heard from others on my party phone line that they suspected I was dealing marijuana. When I confronted him with that rumor on a Tuesday, he suggested that letting him search my house on Sunday would end the gossip. I invited him out. When the sheriff came, we sat on my porch for an hour, drinking lemonade. The rumor died.

Later a high school student was an intern for the school. His parents were very upset, because they told him they had heard our school trips were really sex and drug orgies. Two weeks later he convinced his parents to talk to me. His mother invited me into the living room, his father walking out immediately without a word. I explained to her our trips were not sex and drug orgies. She laughed, and said she knew that, but her real worry was that I would turn her son into a tree-hugger, an environmentalist.

I asked with a look of shock, “Is it worse for your son to be an environmentalist than a drug addict?”

“Yes,” she said, “it is.”

I was called before the local school board by a board member and accused of teaching environmentalism to her elementary school children, citing a lesson in which she claimed my program staff had asked some six-year-olds, “If a coyote lived in a cave with a gold mine, and a miner wanted to mine the gold, who should get the cave?”

As she was talking, a couple of other parents sitting next to her nodded their heads in assent at everything said. As my program staff stood to respond, another parent sitting next to us whispered, “Sit down, let her make a fool of herself.”

The board member read aloud a newspaper article on secular humanism to the other school board members. After she finished, another member said, “What exactly are they teaching your children at their school that you find so objectionable?”

"Animal adaptations, rock types, flower identification ... stuff like that," she stated through clenched teeth.

"Well," he said, "That's exactly what I taught you in high school as your science teacher, so what's the problem?"

The superintendent said, "I just don't see how this outdoor school can have all the influence you say they have, if their program is only in a single grade of our county classrooms for two days out of each school year," and called to proceed to the next agenda item.

The next week a now-defunct local newspaper and the *Salt Lake Tribune* ran articles headlined, "Radical Environmentalism Takes Over San Juan County Schools." I laughed, saved the article for future fundraising letters, and my program continued to work with schools in the county, even with the bullying of this school board member.

Another local right winger wrote a letter to the editor of the other local newspaper, *"How many jobs have been lost to this community and county because of the mystical, romantic environment beliefs that are promoted, encouraged, and taught at the Four Corners School? Make no mistake Ms. Ross is a diplomat and can sell refrigerators to eskimos and talk monkeys out of trees, but her agenda is crystal clear. She wants Southeastern Utah to be WILDERNESS!!!"*

This letter to the editor made me think back to what I had learned from my parents about standing up to bullies! I had no fear and gave them no power over me. I did not take these insults personally, they did not make me feel unsafe, I found humor in them, ignored them, and built support with others in my community, thus a surprising partnership later emerged.

Emma was also bullied about her quilting message when her quilt, Out Where the West Begins, had what some saw as a swastika quilted into its border. She had copied this symbol from Navajo blankets into her quilt. When it was shown at an Arizona state fair, her patriotism was questioned by fair-goers. In response, she pasted newspaper articles in her scrapbooks explaining what the swastika meant to the Navajo people, as she had read they believe it is an ancient symbol with multiple meanings—the four directions of the universe, a progression of thought from ignorance to wisdom, good luck, a symbol of the Great Spirit. Later she created a museum window display of the quilt, the newspaper articles, and a letter about her love for her country.

Dad Pratt wrote to Emma, "Surely I was glad to hear of your success at your state fair ... but I do not wonder after I saw the picture of you and your quilt. It is beautiful in every way ... and I wish you all success in the future." She too did not give bullies power over her.

The seeds that I had planted allowed my place-based outdoor education school to grow, and be accepted by many using science-based arguments. Ongoing research showed that place-based education helps children with nature experiences have greater self-worth; produces student gains in social studies, science, language arts, and math; enhances problem-solving, critical-thinking, and decision-making skills; and builds community engagement. The needle of public opinion tried to pierce me, yet I was protected by a thimble of purpose and place.

THIS BLOCK OF MY LIFE QUILT WILL BE A MAP OF THE COLORADO PLATEAU

Chapter 20

Contemporary Quilting

"Quilts have become, for thousands of women, both an artistic and personal statement reflecting the demands of a society in transition." [25]

Quilting came out of a complex past ... in fact, the "story" in each quilt is an important part of historic quilts, and now contemporary quilts as well. This takes talent (that you are born with) and skill (that you acquire).

THE FIRST FOUR CORNERS SCHOOL OF OUTDOOR EDUCATION story trip was a ten-day backpack trip in March for 12 high school students from an eastern private school, and it was quite cold. Their teacher and I planned to hike 45 miles in three canyons on Cedar Mesa—down Lime Canyon, up

Road Canyon, and down Fish Canyon—each about 1,300 feet deep with cream- and red-striped canyon walls, and full of stacked stone structures of the Ancestral Puebloan people who once lived there. We hiked cross-country, finding our way with no trail out of Lime Canyon and into Road Canyon, teaching the students to read a map and use a compass. We let students lead each day, but cross-country route finding was challenging. Occasionally we came to an impassable dry waterfall in the wash, backtracked and down-climbed elsewhere, until we reached the canyon bottom again. If the students made a mistake, we let them decide how to correct it, intervening only if we perceived danger. After each ten-hour day, we made it to a suitable campsite in a dry wash, continuing our zigzagging journey the next day. We carried enough food, water, and camp gear for five days in our 50-pound packs.

On day six it was time to collect our restock of food for the next five days, left in my truck on the rim. We left eight students in camp by themselves, and with empty packs, two students and my co-leader and I hiked out to my truck. My co-leader and I decided we needed to move the truck four miles closer to a paved road so it wouldn't be stuck if it rained hard, which dark clouds and wind advertised. We sent the two students back, but with this additional four miles to get back to camp, he and I began running to make up time in the remaining daylight, as we now faced a hike of 11 miles back to camp. We dropped back into the canyon just as the sun sank behind a wall of clouds, with three miles left to go. Dark came, and the rain began to fall in sheets that soon turned to snow. We found an overhang out of the flood plain, common in canyon country, and were forced to spend the night. We had matches, so we gathered wood for a fire, changed into warmer clothes, and ate the last of our trail food. The snow began to fall in large flakes; and then water began dripping over the fire and us. We heard the creek rising—tumbling rocks rumbling and crashing. We slept very little. At daylight we set out, and after two hours of hiking in wet, dense snow, and cold water up to our ankles, we neared camp.

Rounding a bend, we saw two students heading upstream looking for us who shouted, "Hello, are you OK?" With an affirmative nod, we all four headed back to our camp. Seeing the group had moved camp higher up, out of the flood plain, we congratulated them on their good judgment and adaptability to the changing weather. Dry clothes and a hot meal were a welcome relief.

The next story trip was for the same private school, its hockey coach and team, on the San Juan River as part of their spring break wilderness experience. It was March, windy, and 45 degrees during the day. We packed 15 dry bags of personal gear, eight coolers and 14 large metal "rocket" boxes (a river runner's term for U.S. Military Surplus PA120 40mm Ammo Can) of food for this ten-day trip. "They eat a lot," the coach emphasized. The first night we camped on a sandy beach at a bend in the river. It blew so hard that every tent had a quarter inch of sand in it by morning. One of the students had shaved his head before the trip so he wouldn't have dirty hair. Every morning he took a bath in the ten inches of cold, chocolate-colored river water near shore, scrubbing his shaved head hard. Each morning the rest of the group got out of their tents, hooting and clapping his cleanliness ritual.

On day five one of them looked up, paused, pointed, and asked, "Are those bunnies up there?" I looked up at a ledge 1,000 feet up the canyon wall, and laughed. "No," I said. "They are bighorn sheep running." By day ten they had eaten everything but one bottle of ketchup. As we neared the takeout we saw that a huge rainstorm had turned it into a sea of mud. One of the students with a load of gear took off toward the gear truck, through what started out as ankle deep mud. A couple minutes later I looked his way and saw him up to his chest in mud. His coach saw him too, threw him a rope, tied it to the truck, climbed in, and towed the mud-encrusted student plus gear to drier ground, congratulating him for his effort.

This outdoor education trip pattern was repeated over many, many more years. In ten years, Four Corners School grew from one trip annually to 45. I guided every trip while running the office and planning different menus for each trip. Standard menus were created, guides hired, more gear bought, and a bigger office set up in town. My home was still basecamp for all trips. Income never quite met expenses. I worked seven days a week, 14 hours a day, which was never enough. I grumbled under my breath when something broke or trips didn't go as planned.

In year 11, I co-led a late fall trip to study polar bears in Churchill, Canada on Hudson Bay. I was to meet the group in Winnipeg, Canada. A chain of events in my flights found me in a plane close to the Winnipeg airport as the train to Churchill was to leave the train station. I told the flight attendant I could not miss the train; it only ran once a week. He nodded in assent. Just before the plane landed the flight attendant asked me to sit in seat number one by the door. When the plane landed he personally escorted me out of the plane, through customs with my luggage, and into a waiting cab—in ten minutes. The cab driver roared through town to the train station. On arrival, he personally ran into the station hauling my duffel. I spotted a conductor and asked breathlessly, "Has the train to Churchill left yet?"

"Are you Janet?" he replied hopefully. "We waited for you for 30 minutes, but we had to let the train go. Go find a cab and wait for me on the curb," he yelled and ran off.

The conductor soon came running out and said, "The train is waiting for you at 55th and Vine. Hurry!" He handed me a piece of paper, saying, "Use this to pay the cab fare."

I looked back and waved thanks, as the cab driver and I sped away. Arriving at 55th and Vine I saw a conductor holding a lantern on the tracks, the train 50 feet away, and my co-leader and group standing on the caboose shaking their heads in disbelief. I jumped aboard and the train jerked forward. My back ached after lugging my duffel from plane to cab to train. It continued to hurt for the entire train ride, even with pain medication. After two days, the train reached Churchill, and we drove to the research station where we stayed for the duration. Our first excursion to see the polar bears the next day was by tundra buggy—a tall, tracked vehicle that held about 25 people. As we sat ten feet up, the bears put their paws up by the windows and looked inside. Camera shutters clicked and clicked. But my back continued hurting.

On a windy, subfreezing day we went to a Hudson Bay beach. It had a giant undulating sponge of sea foam, the result of a high concentration of natural organic matter and constant strong cold winds. It was eight feet tall, 50 feet wide, 100 yards long, and moved slightly with the waves like a very large cube of brown seaweed-smelling Jell-O. Three of us walked inside the foam, completely enveloped in this huge bubble of salty, warm, dark, porous foam mass. We ran out again into the wind and threw bits of foam at those in the group who would not go inside. I felt safe and briefly free of pain.

Home from the trip, I could not walk upright because of my back pain. It hurt to load my wood stove and climb the stairs to my bedroom, so I slept downstairs on a futon couch. My cat Sheba died late one night, and since the ground was frozen and my back hurt I could not bury her. So, I decided to cremate her in my wood stove, by adding wood and tossing her in, and damping down the air intakes (just like Sam Magee of Robert Service fame). A week later I had surgery for a bulged disc, followed nine months later by a hysterectomy. It was time to stop, heal, and reflect on my life and the school, find a new life pattern that was kinder, and not relapse back to a pattern of unsustainable ways, even if memorable.

The first new educational pattern-making course was called "Teaching Environmental Ethics." It provided traditional and non-traditional teachers the skills and knowledge to help their students form an environmental ethic and act on it in their own communities. On one trip, we were at the ranch of friends. The ranchers invited us into their home, fed us, housed us, and provided scholarships. One evening we joined in a circle, sharing our personal environmental philosophies and stories. One teacher said, “I grew up in a ranching family, but now, after seeing what tremendous damage ranching does to the land, I could never be a rancher. In fact, I will fight ranching until my last breath.” The rest of the teachers nodded.

The rancher’s wife retorted, “Do you eat animal products? Do you wear leather shoes? Do you drink milk? How dare you say that my way of life is not as good as yours?”

The rancher began to cry, and others joined her. The next person in the circle said, “You are right. We shouldn’t criticize your life unless we all want to live in caves.”

The group talked into the night about the impact our ever-changing world is having on rural ways of life, and the battles we all fight to maintain compassion for all living things, including people we disagree with. We talked about how hard it is for people to change, once they are rooted in a way of life, and a belief system. I began to see that connecting people of diverse beliefs in an experiential discussion was a powerful tool toward understanding each other, and that understanding diverse viewpoints was a memorable way to change ideas and practices.

Shortly after that, Four Corners School grew two new programs, designed to build a diverse community of people committed to conserving the natural and cultural treasures of the Colorado Plateau through a compassionate blend of place-based and conservation education programs. We built the Canyon Country Youth Corps—an employment, conservation education, and leadership program for 15- to 25-year-olds; the Bioregional Outdoor Education Project-BOEP (later called Place-Based Learning and Teaching Enhances Academic Understanding, or PLATEAU)—a place-based K-8th grade teacher training program; and a smaller version of Southwest Ed-Ventures.

As author Richard Louv said in 2005, *"Part of our task, as a society, is to begin to think in terms of comparative risks ... There are great benefits of a national nature-child reunion ... (and) there are (greater) risks in raising children under virtual house arrest: Threats to their independent judgment and value of place, to their ability to feel awe and wonder, to their sense of stewardship for the Earth – and ... threats to their psychological and physical health."*

Now Four Corners School's students were taught to understand the entire Colorado Plateau landscape, a visible museum of earth history. The school's classes increased new audiences' place-based awareness of the

Plateau's natural systems while developing critical-thinking and decision-making skills to ensure excellence in education, making education relevant to learners, developing a workforce capable of meeting the challenges of the future, and improving the quality of life for communities. In their own words BOEP teachers explained what the school taught them and how it improved all students' knowledge, motivation to learn, and teacher skills:

"*When students ask scientific questions, immersed in the natural world, they are responding to inquiry with purpose. This is powerful for students. It provides opportunity for vivid analogy and makes learning meaningful, as students interact directly with the sources of scientific inquiry. It makes my students enthusiastic about school.*"

Another teacher said that he "*integrated place-based education into his art curriculum by creating a piece of performance art, the annual Christmas play, using animals from the area. His local wildlife (such as mountain lion, fox, and skunk) delivered gifts of wisdom to a baby born on Christmas, a nod to the traditional Christmas play, with Ute cultural aspects added in using the Ute language names of the animals.*"

Another teacher said, "*one of my lessons included understanding watershed flow and conservation.*

Brainstorming water conservation strategies, students traced their human history onto butcher paper and considered their personal and family involvement in water conservation; deciding and illustrating on the paper what strategies could reduce water consumption. She ... also included mapping the Colorado Plateau, as a throw blanket for the community elders."

I was finding my talent, skill, and joy in building a memorable place-based community that changed lives and skills through experiences in nature, reflecting a society in transition. Talent and skill are signature happiness strengths that come in many forms. Everyone has a talent or skill, if given enough encouragement or guidance, and when you find your joy (a genetic set point) you find your talent or develop your skill.

THIS BLOCK OF MY QUILT WILL BE THE VARIOUS LOGOS OF FOUR CORNERS SCHOOL OF OUTDOOR EDUCATION OVER THE YEARS.

Chapter 21

Common Thread

"Quilts made by ... women reflect the diversity of ... the people ... and places they chose to settle ... sharing threads common to all quiltmakers." [26]

FOUR CORNERS SCHOOL USED A SPECIAL THREAD OF PLACE ON the Colorado Plateau repeatedly—the San Juan River—to improve all students' knowledge, motivation to learn, and teacher skills.

When I first crossed it while driving to a trailhead for a Prescott College backcountry class, I was drawn to this brown, slow, opaque thread of waterway. The San Juan River became my home much of the year. It floated my rafts, washed my dishes, and bathed me. It reflected the canyon walls like brown glass. Through my brown sunglasses I reflected on my life, my brown skin, and my sun-bleached brown-blond hair. It was the lifeblood for many species in an otherwise waterless land, human and non-human, including me.

The San Juan River headwaters are atop Wolf Creek Pass in Colorado. There, when temperatures drop below 32 degrees in the fall, many drops of water are suspended in the atmosphere. An impurity in each water droplet forms a freezing nucleus. The temperature drops more, causing many kinds of sharp snow crystals to form—stellars, columns, needles, spatial dendrites, plates, and graupel. The number of degrees above or below freezing, wind velocity, snow movement, and depth in the snowpack influence the shape a crystal first takes and what it later becomes. Depending on weather conditions, crystals change shape all winter long. As for all life, change is inevitable, so it is for snow crystals too. Yet they start as quietly falling crystals, piling up, layer upon layer, into a cold, white, thick stratified winter quilt.

These crystal forces become bound together into a snow batting; with the sky above as the top and ground below as the backing of an ever-changing snowpack quilt sandwich. The top of the snowpack fluctuates up and down in response to deposition, settlement, melting, evaporation, erosion, and sublimation. The snowpack changes as warmth is transferred from the earth and rocks to the snow. The crystals within the snowpack metamorphose as the temperature within warms and cools. Over the months, these layers are stitched together by the needle of freeze-thaw, freeze-thaw. Sometimes their threads break and layers slide away. But mostly they wait for spring. They wait for warmth, for eddy heat conduction to melt them, anticipating their metamorphosis into a seething mass of moving water.

Spring comes, when white snow turns to brown. The ice crystals are altered into a round rolling, boiling, tumbling mass of liquid droplets, picking up dirt and debris as they run downhill. Down they go through the trees, rocks, and soil. Down they go to the river, detoured to towns, faucets, sewers, glasses, car washes, and finally to the river again. Changing shape again, the ice crystals are animal homes, nourishment for living things, and a soft bed for my raft to float. When I row my raft with eyes closed, my body is the needle, pulling the thread of water through the canyon walls with my oars. It makes me happy, this collision of water molecules, negative ions hitting my bloodstream, causing the water to become positively charged, relieving my stress and boosting my energy.

As a brown river, these former ice crystals float lazily through sandy canyons, past stately cottonwood roots sipping brown tea, past stoic rocks, solitary Navajo hogans, and small towns of Navajo families; past bed and breakfasts, past new houses of frame and cinderblock, and past old stone walls left from houses of prehistoric people; past treatment plants that try to clean out their brown-ness. Yet, with little effort they become brown again. The most successful cleaner of the river is a large, 100-foot-high dam that holds back the brown sediment, and the water comes out clear and flowing below it for 20 miles. Yet, soon it is chocolate again. Brown is the color it wants, and brown it will stay. It revels in its freedom to be what it is, to twist in eddies at the base of rocky obstacles.

In the past, left to its own devices, the San Juan dried up in some years. Now, if former ice crystals are melting, summer rains falling, or the government dam operators releasing, the water still comes. Late in the summer the users use more than the clouds put back. Bureaucrats ponder whether they will let the fish downstream of the dam live another year, cities flush toilets, or let me float a boat below Mexican Hat. Without these former ice crystals, some sentient beings will die. If the government bureaucrats choose to not release water, all life forms in this fragile waterway can die, and some might never return.

When water enters the San Juan's deepest canyons, it determines the lives of the fish, bighorn sheep, birds, insects, beavers, frogs, and snakes. When there is enough water in the river, in a final burst of energy, it will twist and turn through the Goosenecks, over Government Rapid, and finally over the silted-in Slickhorn Rapid. Then the river is forced to slow way down and become lake-like. The former ice crystals are transformed into a little water and a lot of ooze, mud, and sand, stopping dead-still at the green-blue delta of Lake Powell 30 miles later. They mill confusedly around at the delta, supporting bird life on their muddy backs, unable to hold on to what's left of their silt-filled load. The San Juan River is no more. The water must travel ever so slowly through the deep, still water of a lake, named after John Wesley Powell, the first white man to float its length when it was a true river.

The former ice crystals are trapped in Lake Powell. The river that channeled its energies to form this redrock canyon has been violated and pushes toward the Glen Canyon Dam, wanting to flow on to its ocean delta, but is not strong enough to defy the will of man. Not yet anyway, but it will find a way ... the former ice crystals' drive to reach the ocean is uncontainable. Finally, they creep through the lake, and join up with the mother river, the Colorado, before spilling through an opening in the dam that holds them back. This is repeated at yet another dam, and another, until eventually they are all used up and can't reach the Sea of Cortez (Gulf of California).

I traveled back to the mountains again in the fall, lay on the ground and cried at their beauty. My tears eventually became snow that fell and piled up for me to ski through, the tips of my skis stitching a perfect line of common thread again through the unblemished snow-white quilt layers, and the water cycle started again. And the next year again ... which motivated me to make this a common thread of place with almost all my students over 32 years to improve their knowledge, motivation to learn, and teachers' skills.

THIS BLOCK OF MY QUILT WILL BE A RIBBON OF WATER FLOWING THROUGH A DEEP CANYON WITH ME ON A RAFT.

Chapter 22

Seams and Pressing

"It has long been believed that quilts ... are among our richest tools in uncovering the lives and experiences of everyday women in an earlier America ... quilts endure and tell a story." [27]

Pressing is the ritual application of heat, pressure, and moisture to make seams lie flat, and tuck smoothly into one another, without wrinkles or puckers. Press often is the rule.

IN MY EARLY YEARS I MADE A RITUAL OF EXPLORING WILD lands in Alaska, Arizona, Wyoming, and Missouri, looking for my "sense of place." For the first ten years after I started the school I spent at least six months a year with

Four Corners School groups on the Colorado Plateau, mostly in Utah, which scientists would say increased my resiliency, and more importantly pressed the seams of a "place" into my life, and that of others improving knowledge, motivation to learn, and skills. The San Juan River was often the place-based theme, but not always.

One San Juan River story began in July when I led 25 65- to 80-year-olds on a five-day river trip, with an almost clear sky, a few puffy white cumulus clouds, low water, the river deep brown from its ever-present silt load. Two members of the group from New Zealand commented on the river's brown color, saying it looked dirty. I explained about desert rivers and their constant sediment load. They looked at me, shook their heads, and left the trip. The temperature exceeded 100 degrees, yet the 23 people that remained climbed into the six orange and blue rafts loaded down with 23 dry bags, eight coolers of food, ten rocket boxes of kitchen gear, and with our six guides headed downriver. The sand on the banks shimmered with reflected heat. We took the participants to pictographs and petroglyphs left by Ancestral Puebloans—rock art of boxy sheep, human figures, flute players, spirals, tracks of deer and bighorn sheep, handprints, and spears—all carved or painted more than 1,500 years ago—explaining how they were made and what they might mean. By late morning, the water fights started, most heartily by my father. There was splashing with paddles, buckets of water thrown, people spraying each other with the bilge pump. Some fell in the river, laughed and swam closer to their "enemies" to grab their buckets. Others splashed with their hands. Everyone was enjoying it, I thought, but when I looked around I saw three men scowling.

"What's wrong?" I asked them.

"That river is dirty, don't throw any water on us!" they growled "These boats go too slow. We rode here on our motorcycles at 60 miles an hour. It reminds us of the military, all this camping stuff. We want to go home. Everyone wants to go home," they shouted.

In blue jeans, undershirts, long sleeved overshirts, and lifejackets, their faces turned redder and redder, with sweat pouring down. We got to camp, had a group meeting to discuss this, and determine if others really wanted to go home. All but the Three Amigos said they wanted to stay on the river. The three men were still scowling, but got in the river and cooled off.

Later, after dark, a small light appeared ten feet over camp. It darted back and forth several times across us and across the river. Many in the group saw it and asked what it was. Was it a firefly, a happiness set point, a tiny unexplainable expression of hope? The next day inexplicably the Three Amigos wore shorts, got wet, and began to laugh with the group. They gradually entered into the ritual of wetness others were enjoying with smiles.

Another San Juan River trip story was a Summer Science Camp, with 22 local high school kids. They were floating along singing "The Ants Go Marching," with one girl in the river near my boat, when I noticed a wild Canada goose swimming toward her, in what I thought was an aggressive manner. Its neck was stretched out, it honked loudly, and moved at a rapid pace. I asked the girl to get back in the raft, she did, and we continued on. The goose went back to her flock. The next day we were in camp when I saw the same goose (at least I thought it was the same goose), swimming toward our camp. She got to shore and walked right up to our camp kitchen, again honking loudly, just like she was having a conversation with us. Then she walked to the edge of the kitchen, did a butt wiggle, and nested down. Her flock floated past and she honked and honked. It sure sounded like, "Come here guys, it's fun over here, join me." The flock floated by with just a glance in our direction, but our goose stayed put in camp. We were not sure what the goose would do, and this bird put us over the BLM group size limit, so we herded her back into the river with paddles. The next day we moved downstream, and when the river ranger pulled into our new camp, I told her the story of the goose.

She said, "I wonder if it's the same goose that was born

ten years ago at the Sand Island put-in and got so used to people that a local took her home and raised her? On many summer mornings she would swim down the river the three miles from their property to Sand Island, get on a raft with a commercial trip, go all the way to Mexican Hat, get on the bus with the guests, and return to Bluff. One day she even hiked up Eight Foot Canyon with the guests, waddling along like a furry, feathered, long-necked dog, and after a time flew back to the river. She waited for the guests to return to the boats, then continued on the boat with them to Mexican Hat, got on the bus, and returned to Bluff."

I said, "It could be, but how long does a goose live? I'll look that up when I get back." So, when I returned home I read that the average lifespan of a Canada goose is 10-25 years. There are reports of geese living to be 30-plus years of age in the wild. So, I called the local goose papa and said, "Your goose is back."

"What do you mean?" he laughed. I told him the story. He laughed again and said, "You know that goose was so bonded to my oldest daughter that many mornings when she was three, my daughter would take one of her mother's fingers, the goose the other, and they would all go for a walk to the river. As a gosling she would swim in our pool and hug my daughter with a giant wing wrap. We called her Goosie and she stayed for about two years and then one winter flew off and did not return. I wondered what happened to her."

"I'm sure it has to be the same goose," I said. "Goosie must have thought my student was your daughter, was not being aggressive at all, but happy to see her old playmate."

"Wow," was all he could say.

In trying to bridge her two worlds, what stories of her human time had this goose been telling the other geese, we can only guess? What stories of her goose time could she tell us, we can only imagine. Bridging worlds between people or people and the wild was a ritual I was developing. I am sure this goose was remembering her life with humans and her friendship with a young girl, uncovering the lives and experiences of an everyday young woman.

Another San Juan River story was of a Jewish summer camp. It was late July, the river level was very low at 280 cubic feet per second (CFS), and daytime temperature was over 100 degrees. The river was so low we could see the bottom, and the normally brown silty river was clear. The ten students were in inflatable kayaks, a rabbi with a Torah and four guides were in heavy oar boats with all the gear. We did not get far the first day with rigging and loading time, and got stuck on rocks 12 times in the first two miles.

When we got to camp, as we were making dinner, the rabbi and the kids got out the Torah and did the first of what was to be a nightly ritual, praying and chanting loudly. By morning the river had come up to 600 CFS. The next night more praying and chanting, and the river came up to 1,000 CFS. Next night, same thing; the river came up to 1,500 CFS, and by the time we got to Grand Gulch to backpack out the canyon there was a big flash flood down the gulch. Water all the way out for us backpackers, and the two remaining river guides took the boats out with 3,000 CFS to float on. Did this ritual of prayer improve our river passage?

The San Juan River was not the only place-based story at Four Corners School. A man I called the "gentle preacher" began attending land-based trips, the first called "Searching for the Northern Boundaries of the Kayenta Anasazi." When I read his medical form, I was concerned. This trip could be tough for an 81-year-old. We planned lots of hiking, up and down steep hills, camping out for six nights. He set off on the first day wearing gloves to protect the thin skin on his hands, fell down often, bled, got deep purple bruises, but never complained. When we found an archaeological site, we photographed it, filled out site forms, and he sketched it. On his sketches, he always added a poem at the bottom of the page. At the end of his second week-long trip later that year, to count bighorn sheep on the south rim of the Grand Canyon, he handed me an envelope. Inside was a poem and a $1,000 check made out to Four Corners School of Outdoor Education. He stared at me with great intent as I read the poem.

> The prudent say with a knowing leer
> "Surely not thinking of him my dear!"
> One foot in the grave and dearie think,
> Of the banana peel on the brink
> And all that you've heard and remember
> Says no good comes of May marrying up with
> December
> Avaunt and phooey, if love is fun
> It's a new year and life's just begun
> (Woman), I love you, you're my life
> By heaven above you, be my wife.

I read it again, and looked at the check. "Are you trying to buy me?" I queried.

"No, no," he cried, "I'll take the check back if you want, but not the intent of the letter."

"Thank you for the check," I stumbled. "I think you are a dear man, but I barely know you and won't marry you." Over ten years, the gentle preacher went on 20 school trips, two a year, ranging from river runs, to excavations of Ancestral Puebloan rock shelters, often accompanied by his little sister, four years younger. He wrote his own "liability release" forms for each trip.

No liability can roost
If Four Corners is accused
I vindicate well in advance
4 Corners from every malfeasance
Four Corners School can do no wrong
That's my legal dance and song
The outdoors is a dangerous place
They've told me that right to my face.
Cobble hits my head? Drop off a cliff?
O forswear legal "but" and "if."
No way I can blame (the School's) bunch
If I should break my neck or coccyx
If strychnine turns up in the lunch
Or stomachache from rot or toxics.
Battle, murder, sudden death-
How'er I lose my life of breath
My heirs and assigns needn't whine
I've signed off every claim of mine.
If I should hap to break a toe
Dropping a Lister book by Flo
Upon it-skip it, let it go,
Lawyers begone and leave it so.

A snarling dog, a skittish horse
So easily thrown off path or course
Shall bring no blame to Monticello
No matter how the lawyers bellow.

He so impressed a travel writer, who was on another archaeology trip he attended in Colorado near Mesa Verde, with his determination, thirst to learn, and his ability to look forward, never behind, that she wrote about him in a 1994 issue of *Odyssey* magazine...

"That's when our oldest and most spirited member, an almost 89-year-old ... retired Episcopal Minister, took a giant step from his slick, mid-stream perch and toppled over into the Mancos River like a bowling pin. Dripping wet, with blood running down one lean leg from a nasty gash, [the minister]—who had been quickly and expertly rescued from his fall by our outfitters—shook himself off on shore. "Let's go see those ruins: I'm ready," he cried, and off he plunged up the steep bank to the red sandstone cliffs beyond. We "younger folks"—ages 30 and up—shook our heads in amazement and plodded on behind this gallant trooper."

At the end of another trip to Chaco Canyon he handed me another poem about our instructor Florence Lister, who with her husband Bob, were noted archaeologists, dedicated educators, and authors of over 40 books on southwestern archaeology...

There once was a woman named Flo
Whose face was all in a glow
When she talked of potsherds
And fossilized turds,
And the special stone works of Chaco.

Then along came a man named Lister
Who among the moonlit ruins kissed her
They dug in the dirt
Where they often did flirt
And later came two little "misters".

O' Florence is one of a kind
She has shared and expanded our minds
She made history come alive
And said it straight with no jive
Then relaxed with a bourbon so fine.

She is our Diva of Kivas
At ladder-top we'd all shout Arriba
All throughout the Southwest
Florence gave of her best
And now we all sure hate to leave'ya.

He got great pleasure from hearing about my travels, and new poems greeted me each time I returned. He celebrated his 90th birthday on his last Four Corners School trip to document rock art and ruins in the Ute Tribal Park, the "other Mesa Verde." Over his life the gentle preacher had marched in demonstrations to protect the right of Planned Parenthood to perform abortions, belonged to the Colorado Governor's Task Force on Migrant Labor, and founded Industries for the Blind. He was a devout Episcopalian who preached the faith of diversity and inclusivity and often found the church confining and sometimes unforgiving. He dove into the world with cheery optimism and openness to the human experience. Two years before he died, he drove into a cement wall at 50 miles an hour. He came out unhurt, and then donated his car to Four Corners School. He died in 1995, after several strokes. I was one of three people who spoke at the memorial service at his church, attended by about 500 friends and parishioners. I read some thoughts, a couple of his poems, and last sang part of a Kate Wolf song:

> You in your elegance and humor filled the room
> Your love and your concern
> Your anger at the injustice of man's narrowness
> and fear

Thank you for being here.

Emma had rituals too; one of which was weekly ever-changing Happiness Museum window displays. Her window displays were like the tip of the iceberg, consisting of items drawn from the entire museum, her imagination, and the landscape around her.

These were the place-based lessons Emma taught me and the school taught others, pressing place memorably and ritualistically into experiences which made everyday people happy. Besides improving knowledge, motivation to learn, and skills, research has shown that places with meaning evoke powerful emotional reactions; places can be more than just physical spaces, including emotional reactions that make us feel complete and "at home" with improved mental wellbeing, feelings of nostalgia, security and survival. For many, the strength of the connection with places manifests through a strong desire, and need, to protect these places for future generations.[28]

THIS BLOCK OF MY QUILT WILL BE THE FIVE STATES THAT FORMED MY RITUAL OF PLACE: AZ, AK, MO, WY, AND UT.

Part Four

USING THE SIX P'S TO PREPARE THE LIFE QUILT SANDWICH

"Quilting refers to the small stitches that hold the three layers of a quilt—top, batting, and backing—together. The best way to learn to quilt is to practice, practice, practice. Your quilting will improve in proportion to the time you spend on it." [29]

Chapter 23

Pieced Borders

. . . .

"While not every quilt needs a border, many quilts are transformed by the frame that a border provides. Choose the border that best complements the design of your quilt." [30]

. . . .

A pieced border, using contrasting or complementary colors, frames each block or the entire quilt, and can be organized into daring schemes.

WITH A NOD TO REINCARNATION, LIVES COME IN YOUNG TO OLD souls, some in daring schemes. A "first-timer" is a very young soul, with little knowledge of life, who seems to be learning things for the first time, often filled with fear or naïve ideas. Older souls are wiser, seem to know more than this life could have taught them, whose borders have more contrasting depth. I can't explain why, but this was on my mind when I walked into a quilt museum in a small town in Oregon with a friend. Two women were sitting at a table chain-stitching a quilt. They looked up when we came in, and greeted us warmly. After 15 minutes of self-touring the museum, I sat down with one woman, and asked how she came to be a quilter. I explained that I was writing a book influenced by a quilter from Arizona, her Happiness Museum, her quilts, and happiness in general.

"Well happiness is for idiots," she said. "You can never really be happy. It's not possible, what with all the work and worries in the world. Quilting was a way to get away from home; my parents were very rigid. There were rules about where we played and where we couldn't. I was never that strict with my boys. I made rules, but if they broke them, well it was OK. Now my boys spy on me. I have to hide up here because they are always driving by to check up on me. So, my pastor asked me the other day if I was happy? 'Happiness is for idiots,' I told him."

In contrast I stated, "Emma found happiness in her museum and through her quilts. I found it through lessons I learned from her about quilting, and her love of the outdoors. I even started a school to educate others about the outdoors." She frowned, silently. A first-timer, I thought to myself.

As my friend and I left this UN-happiness museum, it reminded me of when my (Jewish) mother and I were having lunch with her friend, and apropos of nothing, this woman said to my mother in a puzzled voice, "I was wondering, what does it feel like to be Jewish?"

"Well, what does it feel like to be Christian?" my mother replied quickly.

A full minute later her friend replied, "Just normal, I guess."

My mother smiled and replied quickly, "Well, being Jewish feels 'just normal,' too."

As we walked out an hour later my mom and I looked at each other, and simultaneously blurted out, "A first-timer!"

Later I went out to dinner with a friend to a Utah restaurant that had just gotten its liquor license, and only a few months after waitresses were allowed to offer a customer a drink. The waitress proudly handed us a wine list. It had four categories of wine listed on it—red, white, pink, and rosé. We smiled at each other while looking over the wine list.

The waitress, standing tall and proud, asked us, "Would you ladies like a glass of wine?"

"Yes, I'll have a glass of Chardonnay," my friend replied.

The waitress stated, "Yes ma'am. Would you like the red or the white?"

Covering her mouth, my friend said, smiling, "The white, please." We looked at each other after the waitress left, and simultaneously said, "A first-timer!"

Some scientists think there is a body of evidence that consciousness—at least, in certain circumstances—can survive the death of the body; that life after death isn't necessarily just a fantasy or something to be considered on faith, but can be approached in an analytic way, and that the idea can be judged on its merits, and consciousness can be passed on to another soul.

Toward the end of her own storied life, the physicist Doris Kuhlmann-Wilsdorf—whose groundbreaking theories on surface physics earned her the prestigious Heyn Medal from the German Society for Material Sciences—surmised that late professor Ian Stevenson's work had established that "the statistical probability that reincarnation does in fact occur is so overwhelming ... that cumulatively the evidence is not inferior to that for most if not all branches of science."[31]

To me, Emma was a first-timer who gave away anything to anyone who expressed an interest, expecting it to be returned someday. She trusted anyone who came into her museum and sought her friendship. She accepted all gifts without question, and wrote a thanks and notation in her scrapbook. Life supplied her with wiser souls, such as her adopted family and Arizona Quilters Guild friends, who took care of her, and enabled the Happiness Museum to be her life for 21 years.

How do I plan to piece this new information into my life quilt? Perhaps my attachment to place and its connection to happiness comes from my past lives, or my life experiences with younger and older souls, or from the smells, tastes, touch, and sounds of my senses of place. Or perhaps my attachment to place is just a comforting, happy, and empowering thought.

My senses of place were once experienced on the San Juan River with the Music Man, while he sat in a camp chair near the river's edge looking south across to Navajo land, while I sat on the ground under the sound box of his guitar. He switched instruments effortlessly from guitar, to banjo, to mandolin. As moonlight fell on him, his white hair stood out against the night sky, and a melody he was playing vibrated through me. He played "Land of the

Navajo," and even though it was still 75 degrees, the sand radiating heat from an even hotter day, I shivered. Someone else played a complementary dobro, another a contrasting fiddle. The slow rhythm flowing from his guitar grew joyfully staccato, as he played louder and faster. Laying on the warm sand, the notes seemed to burst from his guitar above me, like a flight of yellow fireflies. At song's end, I headed to my sleeping bag, satisfied, tired, humming the last song.

His music activated my amygdala, the emotional center of my brain, where emotions are responsible for music-to-color associations, based on memories. Studies have shown that music releases dopamine; it gives us the same hit of happiness we would get from making love, a piece of chocolate, or in my case a perfectly ripe summer peach. Research shows that the music we like most profoundly starts with what we hear in our mother's womb. We like what she liked. But later it has a social component from our teenage years. We associate music with experiences we had that were happy, sad, beautiful and what our "group" liked, knowledge of the musician's life, and what the musician's music stands for. As author Daniel Levitin said in his book *This Is Your Brain on Music*, brains and music co-evolved and music is fundamental to our species, perhaps even more so than language. *"The composer has to lull us into a state of trust and security; we have to allow him (her) to take us on a harmonic journey; he (she) has to give us enough little rewards—completions of expectations—that we feel a sense of order and a sense of place."*

I am framed by many place-based songs that unconsciously reside deep inside my cells. A Joni Mitchell song *"I am on a lonely road and I am traveling, looking for something what can it be..."*, a Cole Porter and Robert Fletcher song *"Give me land lots of land under starry skies above, don't fence me in..."*, a Badger Clark and Clifton W. Barnes' song "*Desert silvery blue beneath the pale moonshine...coyotes yapping lazy on the hill...", *or a James Taylor song *"There's a song that they sing when they take to the highway ... Maybe you can believe it if it helps you to sleep, But singing works just fine for me..."* When I hear them I instantly know every word and sing along, which evokes in me a happy emotional state activated in the limbic system. That triggers neurons in my motor cortex, releasing endorphins and oxytocin which in turn lowers my stress and anxiety levels, leading me to tap my foot, and move my derrière.

I am also framed by the place-based feeling and smell of rough vanilla ponderosa pine bark, spicy bitter sagebrush, strips of cedar-smelling juniper wood burning in a redrock canyon campfire, and the taste of a sweet Piñon Pine nut. Smells, tastes, and the feeling of a substance create memories because of tiny chemicals that attach themselves to receptors on my sensory cells, travel to the olfactory area of my brain, and create an emotional response and memory. The place-based sound and sight of a canyon wren singing a scale of descending notes goes into my brain through hair cells called cilia, which produce a series of electrical signals from a sudden burst of acoustic information, and a memory of waking in the morning on the San Juan River. When I see, hear, smell, touch, taste or perform an action, or see others do it, mirror neurons fire, create an image of that action, place it in my memory box, and evoke an emotion associated with that memory that lasts forever.

THIS BLOCK OF MY LIFE QUILT IS 15 MUSICAL NOTES, A PEACH, AND A CANYON WREN.

Chapter 24

Stitched Traditions

....

"The awesome beauty of nature has long inspired quilt artists ... If they capture even a fraction of this inspiration in their quilts, artists complete the circle back to nature." [32]

....

Quilts, and other stitched and woven art forms, are part of daily life in many cultures. Designs used are often inspired by the beauty of a place, which for many people is in nature.

EVERYONE MAKES A LIFE QUILT, WHETHER THEY PLAN TO OR not. To intentionally plan and construct a life quilt is a traditional art form. If one's life quilt is place and nature-based it helps continue the circle of life, the ever-changing inevitable cycle, to which we must all adapt.

This was the focus of several Four Corners School programs to learn about the traditions of the Hopi people in Arizona, one of the Colorado Plateau's several Native American tribes. One trip was to a Corn Dance at Moenkopi, a Hopi village near Tuba City, Arizona. It started with the sun rising behind 30 corn dancer Katsinas, Hopi spirit messengers, as they came out of the kiva in slow single file, the men wearing white woven skirts, the women black woven dresses with a woven white and red cape. The Corn Dance symbolizes a bountiful harvest and also asks for blessings of rain for corn, that is life to the Hopi people, I was told. All the dancers wore moccasins and a shell and bone necklace, and some had red, white, black, and blue wooden and feathered head-dresses and gourd rattles. They formed a circle in the plaza and began to chant and move in rhythm to a drumbeat, shaking their rattles for more than an hour, then went back to the kiva for another hour. Four times this was repeated.

The plaza was empty each time they went back to the kiva, except for a large cardboard box the size of a refrigerator in the center of the circle. When the dancers came out for the first, second, and third rounds they ignored the box, dancing around it, as if it weren't there. On the fourth cycle of dancing, about four in the afternoon, as they went back into the kiva, one of the male dancers went over to the box. He slowly opened one side that had been slit to open like a door, and walked away looking back several times. Inside was a man sitting on what resembled the seat of an outhouse, with his pants down around his knees, kissing a magazine, and whistling at its pictures. Suddenly, the man in the outhouse looked up, saw the audience, pulled up his pants, and ran from the box. Hoots, laughter, and jeers followed him.

At another dance on Second Mesa my group watched from the rooftop another traditionally pantomimed lesson. After a second round of dancers left the plaza, people began to put food in the center of the circle—piles of Wonder bread, soda, juice, fruit, candy, and assorted homemade items like cookies, horno-oven baked bread, and cakes appeared. Then a Koshare (a clown that is part jester, priest, and shaman: part personifying supernatural spirits and controller of society.) He began to pantomime a story, heaping all the plaza food into a big washtub, stepping into the tub, stomping on the food with his bare feet, stepping out in the dirt and back in, walking around the tub adding more food each time, singing happily. When it was all mashed together he stepped out, put some of the brew in a glass, and walked toward the crowd. People ran in all directions. He chased, and finally caught a community member and poured a glass of the stuff down his throat. The man spat it out then stumbled around, lurching and slurring his speech. Hoots, laughter, and jeers followed him.

At another dance at Moenkopi we watched a Koshare search the audience for someone to race. He ran to my father, put a headband on him, and pushed him to the race start. Another community member was put next to him. Tag, and the race began. My father won! The other racer slapped him on the back, gave him some food, and rubbed some cream on his face. My father looked surprised, his eyes watering from the astringent cream. Lots of hoots and laughter followed as my dad walked back to where my mother and I were sitting, with commentary from the audience following him.

"Did you see that Pahana? He was very clever and fast." Another traditionally pantomimed place-based traditional lesson.

When another Four Corners School group went to the Hopi mesas in March, there was a dark snow-threatening sky. We arrived at the motel after lunch and went to a room to prepare the participants for the week to come. "Be prepared to accept new things. Prepare to eat new foods and explore new ideas," we explained. "Be flexible." We spent a few days meeting Hopi people, watching pottery demonstrations, and visiting homes. We ate wafer-thin piki bread, stone-fried bread made of blue corn meal. We had mutton stew, hominy, and bread baked in a horno (outdoor adobe beehive) oven. We walked through villages on top of high mesas, 800 feet above the desert floor. We visited old stone houses heated by wood stoves, with pictures of men in World War II uniforms, family members, Jesus, and John F. Kennedy gracing their walls. Small, shy children darted in and out, sitting on a grandmother's lap one minute, off to find a friend the next. Some families had electricity; some kerosene lamps and wood heating stoves.

One afternoon we were invited to the Hopi tribal chairman's mother's house, who lived on a farm several miles outside of the villages. She took us into her home and showed us yucca plaques she had woven and stored in a garbage can. Most of the plaques had Butterfly Maidens, Crow Mother, or eagle designs—symbolic, she said, of various Hopi spirits. She showed us how she made the plaques by soaking the yucca stalks until they were pliable, then weaving them in and around each other in a spiral fashion. She had made dyes for the yucca stalks by hand from local plants.

We went outside later to make popcorn the traditional Hopi way, placing the kernels in a dutch oven filled with hot sand, and talked about how different our hostess's life was from ours. Our hostess's dog came over to the group. He dragged one leg encrusted in blood, with no foot, covered in maggots. Our hostess began to cry, and told us the dog's foot had been severed in a trap. She asked my co-leader if he would do her a big favor and shoot the dog. My co-leader took her gun and began to cry. Our whole group looked the other way, chins trembling. We turned our backs, shoulders tight, and waited for the gunshot. When it came we jumped, and sobbed with our hostess, who placed an old quilt over him. All of this took ten minutes, no more. We left shortly thereafter as the sun was setting, still sniffling. Going down her driveway, we saw a sheep licking a newborn lamb, no more than 10 minutes old. We all smiled silently through our tears. Death was the scissors that ended the dog's life, but birth renewed the cycle—in a place-based, traditional way.

Traditional place-based images from nature like eagles, flowers, corn, spirit figures, birds, butterflies, and lambs have made their way into many traditional Hopi art forms—baskets, paintings, jewelry, and even quilts. Quilt making was brought to the Hopi people by missionaries, I had read, as an opportunity to proselytize, but the Hopi people made it their own tradition by using cloth flour sacks, used clothing, and un-matched quilt blocks sent to mission churches. Hopi quilts (*tavupu*) have spread into many aspects of Hopi life, as bed coverings, for important rituals—like a Baby Naming ceremony—and sometimes as burial shrouds.

What does a sense of place mean to the traditions of the diverse cultures of the Colorado Plateau? In American English, *sense of place* encompasses the meanings and attachments that places hold for people. Place-based education focuses on local and regional environments and synthesizes different ways of knowing them, leveraging the sense of place of students and teachers as a starting point to teach subjects across the curriculum.

In Spanish, *querencia* is a place on the ground where one feels secure, a place from which one's strength of character is drawn—a place in which we know exactly who we are—the place from which we speak our deepest beliefs. *Querencia* encompasses a sense of self, drawn from a relationship to place, secures the deep feelings that attach self to its community and landscape.

In Navajo, *Diné bikéyah* means land or place of the Navajo people. The land on which the Navajo live is defined and bound by four sacred mountains. Their hogan (house) replicates their "place home" and provides the Navajo with both a sense of place in the universe and a practical home. The Navajo bury their umbilical cord at their place of birth, as a connection to their home.

In Hopi, *Tuwanasavi* means the center of the universe. Their center place is their northern Arizona home, the land to which they were destined to be after many years of migrations around the continents. They were destined to live there as it brought them closer to the earth, surviving in a very rugged and desolate area that provided them with humility and strength.

Each block of Out Where the West Begins, my favorite quilt of Emma's, was stitched with a traditional tribute to her sense of place in her home state of Arizona, with its trademark cactus, rattlesnakes, and blue sky. In a circle at the top of the quilt she had embroidered the state bird, a cactus wren, perched near the state flower, a saguaro cactus blossom. Embroidered in a circle at the bottom was the log cabin in Prescott that served as the territory's first capitol. The co-presidents of the Arizona Quilters Guild awarded Emma the first-ever Arizona Quilt Artisan Award for this and her other quilts, later to become a Guild tradition. Later they published her story in a chapter titled "Beyond the Ordinary—Quilts as Art" in the book *Grand Endeavors: Vintage Arizona Quilts and Their Makers* (1992).

. . . .

"For indeed quilts are more than decorative bedcovers, they are genuine documents that illustrate the generosity of spirit, the strength and creativity of ***all*** *American(s)."* [33]

. . . .

THIS BLOCK OF MY LIFE QUILT IS A MOTHER SHEEP LICKING HER NEWBORN LAMB.

Chapter 25

Strip Piecing

"Color is the first key to originality, then line and design—imagination, even vision. And if the work is not perfect fifty years from now, who will know the difference? Give whatever you decide to make your very best effort." [34]

Strip piecing, or free form piecing, starts with making a quilt design, cutting it into strips, and then reassembling it into a new design.

WHEN I FIRST STARTED FOUR CORNERS SCHOOL, TO GET TO MY home office and basecamp one had to turn south from a paved state highway, then drive seven miles down a narrow but paved road, one more mile of gravel road to my driveway—a narrow dirt road with two sharp bends—before ending at my house. The one mile of gravel road went further south, but eventually became a four-wheel drive road and then a dirt bike path. So, one morning when I heard a knock at my back door at 6 a.m., I ignored it. No one ever knocked on my door let alone at 6 a.m. They continued to knock, so I finally got up, looked down from my second-floor window onto my back porch, and saw an African American woman with a map in her hands. I sleepily asked how I could help her.

The woman looked up and said, "Am I on the right road? Is this the road to Albuquerque?"

I explained that this was a dead-end road, but she held out her map, pointed to where she thought she was, and said that it showed this was the shortest way to Albuquerque. I explained again, more forcefully, that this was a dead end road, she needed to return to the highway and head east, then south. She shrugged and asked sheepishly if there was a place to turn around in my driveway, as she was driving an 18-wheeler. I looked out my front window and indeed she was. I laughed out loud and told her I had never thought to build a semi turn-around, and she would have to back out. It took her 45 minutes, but she did it.

Five years later, I was sitting at my desk looking out at my driveway, and saw a minivan pull up. Its African

American driver motioned for me to come outside. I walked out and up to his window. He too held a map and I asked how I could help.

"Is this the road to Albuquerque?" he replied.

"No," I said and grabbed his map. "You are the second person to ask me that, so I have to ask, is there an African American AAA that gives out bad maps?"

I showed him where he actually was on his highway map, a small dead-end road off a two-lane road. I told him how to get to Albuquerque, perhaps a bit harshly.

"Ok ... Ok lady," he barked, thanked me, and drove away quickly.

In a county with maybe two African American residents, this was an unusual occurrence. Perhaps it was meant to direct me down a path of working with diverse audiences in my school, as over 50 percent of the county is Navajo, and by exploring their needs could build programs to serve them as an agent of social change.

Several years later I co-led a Four Corners School trip to Canyon de Chelly. We hiked down an obvious trail from the north rim of the canyon overlooking Spider Rock, home of Spiderwoman, a tall spire that pierces the sky like a red needle, was our destination. We stopped for a rest break and encircled our Navajo guide as he told of his childhood, and the boarding school a few hours away that tried to take away his identity. "Tradition is the enemy," read a plaque on his school wall. He was not allowed to speak his native language at school; his long hair was cut as they considered it unsanitary. He was seldom allowed to visit home. "How can you still live here happily?" I asked in shock. His answer was:

> In Beauty—happily I walk
> With Beauty before me I walk
> With Beauty behind me I walk
> With Beauty above me I walk
> It is finished in Beauty.

His family, language, and culture were the most important things to him, he said. He used his "jish," a deerskin prayer sack, his prayer sticks, flint arrowheads, and corn pollen to connect to his earth mother. He traced the shape of his footprints in the earth and sprinkled them with corn pollen to walk in. He told us the Navajo creation story—of the Blue World, the Yellow World, the White World, and the Black World. All four worlds were tied to the four directions he said, and the four sacred mountain ranges that border and frame the Navajo Nation—the same mountain ranges I see from my home. He explained there are parts of one's past to keep, and parts to put to rest.

We continued to hike hard the rest of the day, up and down ravines, under trees, and through red-hot dirt. He was often so far ahead we could not see him, so we just followed his tracks, as there was no formal trail. It was around 100 degrees, and heat waves shimmered above the ground. We *Belaganas* (Navajo for Anglos) hiked on, plodding in the footprints he made for us on the red dirt, through piñon and juniper trees. The sun sucked moisture from our fair, white skin and turned us red, but we followed our guide's good sense of the land. We feared he was lost, as he had no map or compass. A participant at the front of our group lost sight of our guide's footprints denoting the trail to follow.

"Which way do I go?" he asked me, as I was just behind him.

"Just follow the footprints," I replied.

He stumbled forward, veering off the obvious path with footprints.

"To the right," I said. "Through the bushes."

For a moment we were on the trail again, then went astray once more.

"I can't find the trail," he complained, "you lead."

"Focus your eyes, "I explained. "Follow the footprints."

He tried but lost the path again, in a few hundred yards. So, I led. My attention was divided. I looked up to see what was coming, so as not to bump into a branch or rock. I looked down to see the path, our guide's footprints, and animal tracks. Look up, look down, up, down—this dichotomous view got us to our guide. Our guide's planning and sense of place brought us full circle and we arrived safely back at the truck at 4 p.m. I had left a watermelon in the cooler on ice. I passed around thick slices, and everyone took big bites, juice dripping down their chins, spitting seeds into a stiff breeze. We slurped, and said little while sucking down the pink, wet, sweet flesh. Like cactus, we swelled to store this moisture, smiling, and laughing out loud.

I wondered to myself, why is it so hard to follow a trail? Am I following the right trail for the school? And then unexpectedly, twenty years after I started Four Corners School, the city fathers—the people who had always been suspicious of me and the school—asked me to partner in building a science center. The path I had been following never led me to a goal of building a facility. Four Corners School was always about field-based activities. But, I stated flatly to those asking to partner, if they wanted a science center that taught creationism, I would not do that. If they wanted dutch oven cooking and cowboy poetry as its focus, that was not for me either. They laughed, and so did I! I began to understand the life cycle of any non-profit, to see the inevitable need for changing the design of the school, if I and it were to survive and thrive. I thought, life is not about always sticking with the assumed or easy path, it is about making a difference, accepting a challenging path, sometimes taking apart your first plan, and free-form piecing a new one from a new perspective.

I took the opportunity offered, yet continued to wonder if I should have followed this new trail, or simply continued on the familiar one? How would I like it, embrace it and manage it? Any opportunity offered and taken, or not, is a future investment, has a cost, and the cost is not chump change. Over the next 13 years Four Corners School, with the help and support of the community, followed a new and winding trail whose path was clarified through three scoping meetings, a Market Feasibility Study, 40 community leadership team meetings, 20 informational meetings, eight science mini-events, a business plan, a donor study, and finally a capital campaign to make certain that a place-based Science Center was not only likely to succeed, but would meet the unique needs of the local and larger constituent community, create a new campus for the school, and new future for Monticello city.

THIS BLOCK OF MY LIFE QUILT WILL BE TWO MAPS AND A COMPASS.

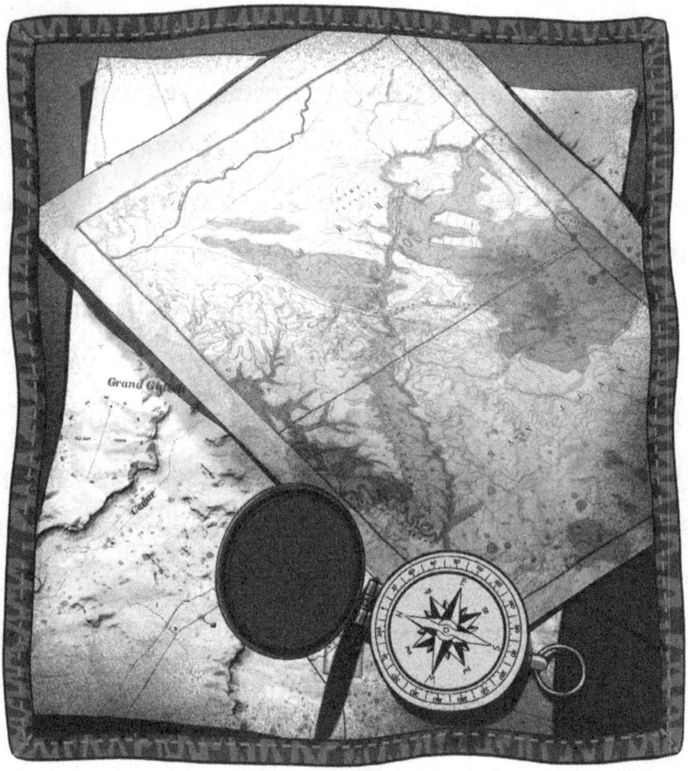

Chapter 26

Scissors

"Quilts have been a high-spirited artistic expression of American women over the past two hundred years..." [35]

Quilts take time, and scissors become important tools (or lethal weapons) in the hands of thoughtful or overzealous needle workers.

WITH A NEWLY INSPIRED VISION (TO BUILD A DIVERSE community of people who are committed to conserving the natural and cultural resources of the Colorado Plateau, through hands-on engagement in placed-based programs) and a new **mission** (to create lifelong learning experiences about the natural and cultural treasures of the Colorado Plateau for people of all ages and backgrounds through conservation, adventure, service, and education programs), new programs were created for new place-based audiences to teach a lot more about the Colorado Plateau bioregion, where all our programs took place.

Frank Traina and Susan Darley-Hill, in *Perspectives in Bioregional Education* wrote, *"a bioregion can be described as an area without hard boundaries ... distinguished by its many natural features including the flora, fauna, soil, climate, geology, and drainage area. A critical component of a bioregion is the human culture, which has developed within and is integral to that area ... In short, bioregionalism is having, or developing 'a sense of place.'"*

Participants were helped to shape their own sense of place from the school's new programs. As told to me by one Canyon Country Youth Corps (CCYC) crewmember whose life was changed by his place-based experience, *"The crew really got me interested in becoming a wildland firefighter. I went back to school after that crew was completed with a new strength to finish school so that I could move on with my life. If it was not for Four Corners School, I don't know where I would be now. I have graduated high school; I am living drug free and I will be going to Wisconsin to work for my uncle as a lumberjack. I am planning on getting a job next year as a wildland firefighter. It changed my life."*

Another CCYC member said of his place-based experience, *"It was an experience that opened my mind and helped me to learn more about myself and the environment. It was very life changing."*

A Bioregional Outdoor Education Project (BOEP) teacher whose skills and enthusiasm for teaching were improved said, *"Because of your program I am enthusiastic about place-based education and am now viewed by my peers as an expert and resource on bioregional outdoor education at school. I have a lot more confidence in teaching in general. I have changed my whole philosophy of teaching to include helping my students appreciate and understand their local environment of the Colorado Plateau."*

A Navajo BOEP teacher said she had helped her students raise test scores: *"The Bioregional Outdoor Education Project has been a great success in my classroom this school year. I can see the difference in all test scores taken in the Kindergarten classes in my district. My class has the highest scores in the district because of what I learned in the program.*

A Southwest Ed-Ventures trip participant said of her improved motivation and happiness in life, *"my favorite Four Corners School moments; many so deep, they've found a permanent home at my core. They live in me, and flow like a mighty river in my veins. The ... moments are the source of my inspiration, the visions I go to when I think I can't go on, or am leery to try. Since going on the first trip, the girl who was kind of scared, unsure of herself, and lacked any faith in her physical strength is gone. She has been replaced by someone who knows herself well, has gone on to lead others to the outdoors, the river, the path—wherever that may be. She's not really afraid of anything anymore, and has summoned more grit and tenacity that she ever dreamed possible. I don't think anyone can really understand that gift until walking in those shoes, shedding that old skin, and coming into their own, like an idea whose time has come. The best I could do is encourage others to take that journey, whatever trip that may be, and know that the friendships made, the lessons learned will become the fabric of their Soul."*

Emma had once told me to give great thought to my artistry, to the whole image, quality, design and construction of any quilt, not just individual blocks. Long after she passed away, I knew she would have been proud that my life was well-planned, and that I did not use scissors too much or too little.

The 130,000 square miles of the Colorado Plateau, one

of the richest repositories of diverse native plants, humans, and other animals in the U.S., and one of the largest remnants of wild lands left in the U.S., was the perfect place-based classroom for Four Corners School. It was on this canvas that I planned and created happiness for myself and others beyond the ordinary and into the realm of art, from a belief that life need not follow the easiest path to be a true agent of social change.

THIS BLOCK OF MY LIFE QUILT WILL BE A SCISSORS AND SEVERAL BLANK QUILT BLOCKS.

Part Five

ADAPTABILITY TO INEVITABLE CHANGE QUILTS A LIFE TOGETHER

"How many times have you gasped with delight on seeing a beautiful quilt? Walking up to examine it closely, though, has perhaps proved that it was not perfect by any means; you've said to yourself, I can do as well as that—I'm going to try it!" [36]

Chapter 27

The Frame

....

"In creating a quilt, you automatically become a designer, a fabric sculptor ... So get up ... dig out those boxes of pieced squares, and apply them to the world (of quilting) ... and see what kind of motion your fabric imitates." [37]

....

A frame holds fabric stationary, straight, and taut while quilting the final layers together. Finding and keeping a happiness framework is influenced by many interconnected experiences from the fabric of life; like environment, chance, choices, and genetics.

I THINK THAT EVERY PERSON INHERITS A FIXED HAPPINESS SET range or framework from their parents. But variables, such as the region where you live (**your place**), your social network (**friends, love, family, and work**), faith (**spirituality**), and **humor, planning, and adaptability to change,** can push the upper end of your set range. Scientific evidence concurs that people have a genetic set point, or fixed range for happiness, and that humans can learn to find the upper end of that set range, by choices they make. Other scientists would tell you happiness is based on your personal set range, plus the circumstances of your life, and factors under your voluntary control.

A happy or unhappy disposition is thought to be something that can be pushed to its upper or lower end by choices such as **love**, that is activated in two parts of the brain: the ventral tegmentum and the nucleus caudatus—parts of the brain's reward and motivation mechanisms. The brain has a similar response to love, as when one views art or listens to music. Love and music are basic instincts that run along the known neural pleasure circuits and create significant dopamine secretions. Religion-neutral **spiritual beliefs**, experiences, and interpretations are not controlled by the product of a single gene but are complex, involving many genes, each making a small contribution to the phenotype, combined with a very strong environmental influence.

Experiences within the natural world, and our "**place**"

in it, also affect where we are in our happiness set range. Settings that combine "prospect and refuge" influence a sense of well-being. Some people like to live on a hill, or where they cannot be seen by a predator who seeks prey. Water, low canopy trees, and animals in our home are all attractive features for our biological need to satisfy thirst, shade, companionship, and livable habitat. Other research shows that patients in a room with a view recover more quickly and, after a stressful experience, people who watch images of natural landscapes calm more quickly. Other scientists write that we are hard-wired for survival and reproduction, which is enhanced by a prime location or place. Research has recently shown that nature experiences are useful as a therapy for ADHD, and increase children's resilience to stress and adversity. Studies also show access to outdoor experiences reduces crime and delinquency.

Finding one's "sense" of "a" place requires billions of nerve cells to flash urgent place-based messages along cross-linked pathways in the brain. This sensory pathway goes from the thalamus to the cortex, a dynamic pattern processor and organizer, to higher regions in the brain for further definition. Audio, visual, tactile, olfactory, and taste patterns link up with the motor systems that control actions leading to knowing one's "**place,**" whether outdoors or indoors.

Scientists also believe that **humor** ensures you live a longer and healthier life, with more joy and satisfaction, and can be contagious. An automatic reflex to imitate another's expression becomes a mirror, a bridge between people. When someone mimics the expression of a smile, they may also begin to feel more positive. Laughter may have nothing to do with humor, but is an instinctual survival tool for social animals, a way to get along. Scientists call it a behavioral fossil that shows what all humans, maybe all mammals, have in common. The brain has ancient wiring to produce laughter, so young animals learn to play with one another and stimulate euphoria circuits in the brain, reassuring other animals they are not fighting, thus weaving an effective social fabric. Because we share these positive genetic traits with most mammals, certainly they are part of our family.

Researchers think that **planning** is a signature strength used to ensure survival. By planning, you learn from the mistakes of your past, take risks, make new mistakes, and learn again. Yet all reptiles and mammals share a **resistance to change**, scientists say. Our brain feels terror at adapting to new rules of the game, losing control of established customs and traditions. The brain's hippocampus and amygdala, the place where cells are modified and changed, is designed to help us learn new things. Memories are produced by plastic electrical discharges, nerve cells form new interconnections, new protein molecules, and communications made between neurons, enabling passage of information between cells on a regular and inevitable basis.

Other scientists believe that the psychology of joy can be taught like one might teach a trade, that happiness is found by examining negative assumptions, savoring positive experiences, and managing the yearning for more or developing one's strengths and putting them to positive use. Other researchers believe that human beings have a median forebrain bundle, and that if you stimulate it with an electrode you will be happy. Another study suggests there are seven brain molecules that make you feel happy: endocannabinoids (the bliss molecule); dopamine (the reward molecule); oxytocin (the bonding molecule); endomorphin (the pain-killing molecule); GABA (the anti-anxiety molecule); serotonin (the confidence molecule); and adrenaline (the energy molecule).[38] Produce any of these brain chemicals through your daily life choices—like getting regular exercise, completing an important task, meditating, or doing yoga—and you will be happier.

Scientists have found that the human brain is very plastic and evolves in response to experiences through the establishment of new neural connections, the strengthening of existing connections, and the creation of new neurons in the hippocampus. If your environment is enriched, these connections and neurons can increase. On a daily basis those who feel joy, altruism, enthusiasm, energy, social skills, and spirit show more activity in the left prefrontal cortex of their brain, while those who report emotions such as depression, pessimism, anxiety or feeling withdrawn show more activity in the right prefrontal cortex of their brain.

The World Database of Happiness is an archive of research on the subject of happiness, in various languages, from the viewpoints of many nations, collected in a virtual happiness museum.[39]

In many countries where citizens trust their government, happiness is legislated successfully. Bhutan, a small country in the Himalayas, recognizes the supremacy of gross national happiness over gross national product. In Bhutan they believe that improved quality of life for their citizens comes from balancing cultural and environmental preservation. It is the only country in the world where hunting and fishing are banned, and 60 percent of the nation is required to remain forested. There is no destitution or homelessness, education is free, and all families can meet their basic needs with the help of a compassionate government.

Denmark is often called the happiest country in the world, with high taxes to pay for free college and social services, and lots of vacation time. People trust each other, have relatively high wealth, freedom, a good work/life balance, a well-functioning democracy, and work that values the worker.

In Ireland a doctor I met believed that the purpose of government is to be compassionate to its citizens by providing affordable health care. When people are not stressed to meet their basic health care needs, it changes society, making a country and its communities happier.

Americans are more challenged to find and keep happiness. Even when the United States economy improves, happiness among adults does not always follow. Credible explanations include declines in social capital and social support, distrust of government, increases in obesity and substance abuse, increased screen time, decreased sleep, and decreased outdoor time. And in 2020 and beyond, the COVID-19 pandemic and collapsing economy, of course, have been the biggest factor.

In most industrial countries, economic prosperity is equated with happiness. In 2012 the United Nations General Assembly adopted a resolution declaring an International Day of Happiness to be observed March 20th of every year henceforth, which recognized happiness as a "fundamental human goal" and called for "a more inclusive, equitable and balanced approach to economic growth that promotes the happiness and well-being of all peoples." The 2020 World Happiness Report stated that, *"institutionally, building a government that is trustworthy and functions well, and culturally, building a sense of community and unity among the citizens are the most crucial steps toward a society where people are happy ... each country must follow its own path. If citizen well-being and happiness are truly the goals of government, then taking seriously research on institutional and cultural determinants of citizen happiness is the first step in starting an evidence-based journey toward fulfilling that goal."*

Plato believed that happiness was the opposite of pain, and both a physical and mental experience of the soul. Others believe happiness comes from pure chemistry, not circumstances. Some say our happiness comes from an amalgamation of nature and nurture. I believe happiness comes from a blend of pure biology and cosmic serendipity, some of which we can simply recognize, and some of which we can manage, if not control.

In my college days I visited a church an hour from Prescott, in Skull Valley—the Church of the Divine Healing. Friends had said it was a beautiful building, and the minister was very wise. They said I would learn things that could frame the rest of my life. I imagined a brick church with a steeple, altar, and everyone dressed in their Sunday best.

The next week friends and I drove to the church, located in a wide grassy valley, with no other buildings nearby. It was made of rough-cut pine, built around a large pink granite altar boulder, that was half outside, half inside the building. We walked in quietly, as the sermon had started. There were 20 people in pews all wearing jeans, sneakers, and T-shirts, listening intently. I limped to my sea, because of a sprained ankle. The minister did not look up. While he spoke about healing individuals and the world at large, a small mouse ran up and down the pink granite altar boulder. Every once in a while it stopped, cocked its head listening, wiggled its very large ears, and ran out the crack where the wood and rock met. When it returned, it had grass, seeds, or twigs in its mouth, which it took down a hole in the floor to its assumed living space, then ran outside again. Clearly, it felt right at home here.

When the sermon was completed, the minister asked if anyone in the congregation had anything physical or emotional to heal. I raised my hand. "You sprained your ankle," he said before I could answer. He asked me to come forward, and laid his hands on my ankle, which immediately felt better. I thanked him and watched while several more people had a similar experience, then went back to my seat to watch the mouse eat a small seed it held with both paws clasped together tightly. I went to the church several more times. Each time the minister knew if anyone in the congregation was in pain, and helped them come away with a smile. Like comfort food; being there made me feel better, thoughtful, and more peaceful, but was it really my form of faith? After three or four times I stopped going, but appreciating its idea fabric, told Emma about my visits.

"It was interesting," I told her. "He just knew my ankle was sprained, without my telling him. Friends who have been there tell me the same thing. The church is so beautiful, so calming, and built to incorporate the natural world. I am going to call it the Church of the Great Outdoors."

"Belief and faith work in mysterious ways," she said.

"True," I said. "A Navajo person once told my mother her finger was crooked because she had pointed at a rainbow, which could anger the gods. But in my culture, if you see a rainbow, it's good luck and there is a pot of gold at the end of it. Which is right?"

Emma just smiled and said, "Rainbows are made of contrasting colors that frame the sky, like contrasting colored fabric that frames each individual quilt block, and makes a design unique."

Science says rainbows form from a chance meeting of water droplets and light at the same time and at the right angle. They also form when two conditions come together by chance—sunshine at your back and rain in front. When the colored arch is seen, sunlight is reflected from the back of thousands of individual water droplets at angles that your eyes see as color, repeated in raindrops all around you. If you are standing high enough (+20,000 feet), with the sun behind you, a rainbow will appear as a full circle—a very rare occurrence. Chance, the happening of events without apparent cause or design, is the random variable in the rainbow's formation equation and a frame that makes sense to me. Faith, such as unquestioning beliefs that do not require evidence or proof, like the commitment in a Supreme Being, makes no sense to me. Every Supreme Being cannot be the "best", as they are all equally quirky and often used as an excuse for racism, war, and violence. My frame is best suited to scientific explanations, even if a chance event is a part of their creation.

My faith, and Emma's, though contrasting, were the frames that held our lives together. Emma once told me, "The Good Shepherd is my lifeline. Sharing the Good Shepherd is my ministry. It's a sermon in itself—you don't have to say any more."

"I don't believe in a God," I answered slowly. "Or at least not in an all-powerful human-like puppet-master. Formal religion is often an excuse for hatred. But I do have faith in the outdoors, in my sense of place in it, and the natural world that supports us all. I don't believe that faith is a 'sorting hat' for who lives and who dies, or who gets the most stuff. My faith is in science, in facts that require proof. My faith is in Mother Nature and how she supports all living things equally, adjusting as needed, and that all living things have the same basic need to survive and be happy in an interconnecting web. And that I have to continue to work to protect my 'place' through the educational and legal process—where learning leads to knowledge, to understanding, then to concern, and finally to action. I believe that sense of place is essential to finding happiness from a blend of pure biology and cosmic serendipity, some of which we can simply recognize and some we can manage, if not control. "That is my life's framework."

SO, THIS BLOCK OF MY LIFE QUILT WILL BE A RAINBOW AND A MAP OF BHUTAN.

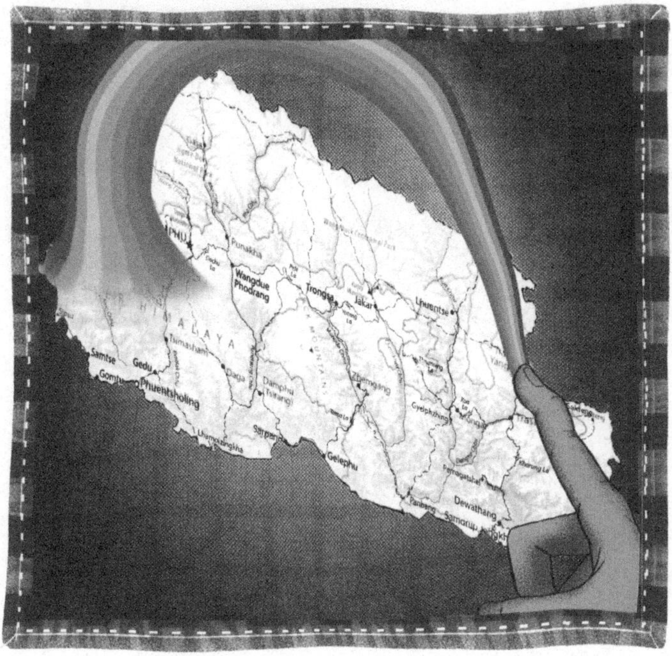

Chapter 28

Chronicles in Cloth

"Wrapping a loved one in a quilt and burying them in a grave ... add to the storehouse of sentiment and emotion attached to the quilt." [40]

Women have always made special quilts to commemorate notable personal events. Many of our earliest childhood memories involve quilts and tell family stories, like Grandma's favorite quilt she wrapped you in while you snuggled in her lap.

MY MOTHER HAD GIVEN ME MY GRANDMOTHER'S HAND-CROCHETED afghan quilt—a rainbow of colored yarns all crocheted into a black background—and told me the story of her mother making it for a granddaughter someday. Lying under it I dreamt of my grandmother, snuggling in her lap, seeing sunlight reflected from thousands of individual water droplets, repeated in raindrops around me, the sun at my back, and a rainbow around me in a full circle.

When I laid under Grandma's quilt, I felt our family generations stitched evenly together by her, the yearnings, joys, hopes, ambitions, and fears of the many women whose genetic recipes I carry, and hope to measure up to with no visible gaps. I hoped that the neural circuitry in my brain made new pathways in my gray matter, as well as new happy conversations. I hummed a Shaker song, *"Tis a gift to be simple, tis a gift to be free ... And when we find ourselves in the place just right, it will be in the valley of love and delight..."* and on a cellular level I knew why music is better than language for expressing feelings.

I had other quilts stored in my closet: a crazy quilt of multicolored fabric with a green border, and a diamond quilt of red, blue, black, pink, and brown with a black border, worn from use, tattered and frayed. Lying under my grandmother's quilt again, I dreamt about how to finish my life, and what I wanted to be in the next one: the Pinto Bean Queen, a bluegrass singer, banjo player, figure skater, or wild horse. It was then I decided to just be content in this life to give back to the world, treat all people equally, and remember to tell loved ones how I feel every day.

My grandmother's afghan covered me again after my mother's death. Tears of sadness and love became an endless chain of stitching together our multi-lineage shared cells in my body, heart, and brain. She lived a vibrant and happy almost-87 years, with the love of many, the end coming while on her 65th wedding anniversary river boat cruise with Dad, in a bathroom 1,000 miles away. So quick, and unexpected. After her heart beat 3.4 billion times, 2.5 billion of them right along with mine, it just stopped. An Express Mail box with the words "Cremated Human Remains" on the outside was left by the postman between the screen and front door of her home. Inside was a black plastic box of bone chips and ashes, the finality of all that was left of the essence of almost 63 years of being my mother, a selfless, loving woman who always sacrificed her wants and needs for the wants and needs of her family. One hundred forty pounds in life, four pounds in death, of her unique elemental composition. Just like that, primary love was gone. It makes sense that my neural circuits were misfiring and dopamine secretions low.

She would want me to continue on with what makes me happy. She had always said to count my blessings. I will always count her as a blessing, and carry happy memories of her in my cells: going down the San Juan

River, sharing favorite books and clothes, her endless storytelling with puppets and costumes, teaching Four Corners School classes together, and laughing so hard at a joke we could not stop. I will add our story of love to my chronicle in cloth.

This was repeated after my dad died five years later, at age 98. After his heart beat 3.9 billion times, 2.7 billion of them right along with mine, it just stopped. His big beautiful heart. His death was not so quick, quite expected, yet still heartbreaking. He was writing his third and final book right up until two months before he passed in a nursing home. Many of his friends have said he was more vibrant than anyone they knew. He was a force of nature, a charmer, full of life and humor, with the highest integrity, dignity, and intelligence—always trying to make the world a better place by building affordable housing for all, working for equitable city planning, volunteering for the Democratic Party, and by writing our family history.

He was passionate about the outdoors, Four Corners School of Outdoor Education, and came to share my sense of place. Together, we explored, hiked, rafted, back-packed, and cross-country skied much of the spectacular public lands and waters of the Colorado Plateau. He was on the School's Board of Directors for 36 years. He and I traveled to many parts of the U.S. and the world together, including Japan, Africa, Alaska, Ireland, Scotland,

Canada, France, and Mexico. We even backpacked 53 miles on the Chilkoot Trail when he was 83.

He was the happiest person I knew all of his life, and a role model for me. His last physical therapist at his nursing home wrote after the COVID lockdown started:

He's fast approaching 100, a long life well lived
Though the corner just turned, says he's got little left to give
A historian, bookworm, papers piled high on his desk
Until he finishes a project, his intellect may never rest
But get him in the pool, he'll make you chase him down
Just like in his mid-twenties he suddenly becomes pound for pound
Humor is his strength, he takes most obstacles with jest
For bringing light into the air, he is one of the very best
I pass his room once more, continued slumber, his room is dim
I wish his family could be here, and in these next few weeks or months, enjoy him.

For three months before his death I could not see him due to the COVID pandemic, but was allowed to be with him for his last five days. I read to him, talked to him, and held his hand. On his last day, I played his favorite music, by Bing Crosby and Frank Sinatra, while he was seemingly unconscious. I began moving his fingers in time to the tunes, and it seemed that he was moving his fingers in time with mine, as they say music is one of the last things you hear before death. I will hold on to that memory of those last few happy days together.

A wooden box of bone chips and ashes was handed to me by the mortuary, the finality of all that was left of the essence of almost 68 years of being my father, a selfless, loving man who was my best buddy, and loved many of the same things I did. He was a kind and generous father to me and many of my cousins and friends. One hundred sixty pounds in life, four pounds in death, of his unique elemental composition, just like his life. I was lucky to have shared his life story as long as I did. Lucky to have a genetic disposition to want to have a mission-based life, which he wrote of in both his books—the first about our family's role in winning the Civil War, and his relatives' continual re-enlistment based on their deep commitment to end slavery; and the second about his great aunt who was a Presbyterian missionary school teacher in the San Luis Valley of Colorado in the 1800s and waged a gentle war for souls with the Catholic Church.

Studies have shown that the loss of a father is more often associated with the loss of personal mastery—vision, purpose, commitment, belief, and self-knowledge. For me it was the opposite, it just motivated me more—even though it happened after I retired—to dive into my projects with the Democratic Party, reinventing the education system with a diverse group of educators, writing, and Rotary service projects on the Navajo Reservation part of our county.

After both of my parents' deaths I cried a bucket of tears, shed a mountain of deficit signals, hugged a basketful of memories close. It helped me find comfort to look around my house at the memory tokens of my life. Some are from a simple, yet magnificent childhood ... a driftwood bird, a gravy pitcher, syrup bear, bronzed baby shoes, photos, girl scout merit badge sash, pictures of the Missouri farm ... Others are from my rich adult life ... a small fossil rock carved with the head of Medusa and yin/yang, photos, sand paintings, Navajo rugs, Salvador Dali print, art work, endless books, and musical instruments, CDs and tapes.

Grief—in its most basic form—represents an alarm reaction set off by a deficit signal in the behavioral system underlying attachment, writes psychology professor John Archer, of the University of Central Lancashire. Death is a part of life that one must allow to take its course in its own time.

Their deaths made me want my remaining years to contain worthy elements that my parents and I will be proud of. For my remaining years I want to still be of value, my life's work continued on, my part in it honored. Since my completed life quilt will be the final bedcover in my home place, a witness of sorts, I want my remaining time to be happy and productive, so when my energy production ceases, my heart stops, and I cannot process any more oxygen or nutrients in my hundred trillion cells, my last stitches are well done.

I worry that some people may not understand why this place brings me such happiness and why I made the choices I did, with no fully evolved partner or children to witness my worthiness. I worry about the bullying I have encountered. I was asked many times by friends, "How can you still live here happily?" I answered with the same prayer I learned from my Navajo friend:

In Beauty—happily I walk
With Beauty before me I walk
With Beauty behind me I walk
With Beauty above me I walk
It is finished in Beauty.

I have learned along the way that chronic worry and stress can trigger a host of health problems. When excessive fuel in the blood isn't used for physical activities, the chronic outpouring of stress hormones can have serious physical consequences: like suppression of the immune system, digestive disorders, muscle tension, and short-term memory loss.

Emma worried, too. She worried when she loaned her favorite antique chandelier to a museum in Prescott that it might never be returned, especially after she saw it hanging on permanent display. She worried that her adopted son might give her quilts to the same museum, and they would lock them in the basement, never on display again. She worried that people did not like her window exhibits.

She confessed to me one day in the museum, "Sometimes I get discouraged and wonder why I am doing my window displays. But then I think, Oh, that's the devil talking. A few people criticize the windows, but I've offered it. I'm sharing."

"Many people in town, including me, are fans, official window watchers," I assured her again. She smiled, a tear sliding down her cheek.

My Prescott friends had told me that just before her Happiness Museum closed in 1984, Emma was honored with the first Arizona Quilter of the Year award. They told me soon after, her quilts were taken down, vacuumed, rehung for photographing, and packed for an exhibit in Phoenix and an interview with the *Arizona Daily Sun*.

When the reporter ran out of questions, friends supplied some. When Emma ran out of answers, they prompted her memory with details they knew. Her friends said they had not seen her so "on" in a long time. She laughed, joked, hugged them, and her red cheeks beamed all through the interview, like valentine hearts. With help, she remembered every detail and story of every quilt and friend she had made through quilting. It was one of the last times in her life she *tied* everything together—in a bold, vibrant display of happiness, personality, history, and craft. Some friends took her to lunch, other friends couldn't bear to help that day. They knew the museum would never be open again. Her adopted son wanted to keep it open, but knew Emma was too old to participate, and he had his own job. So, he boxed up her dolls, thimbles, quilts and items from her museum for sale or storage. He hired a manager for the estate sale and left town while it happened. He kept 20 quilts, some boxes of plastic flowers, all her scrapbooks, and a few other items from the museum.

In Emma's final years her adopted family could no longer care for her, so they put her in a nursing home. She became angry and forgetful. She did not remember her friends and cried easily. The home asked her adopted son to move her, as she was too difficult. He moved her to several other nursing homes and the same thing happened. He finally moved her to the Pioneer Home—two blocks from the Sharlot Hall Museum, to which her adopted son had permanently loaned some of her quilts for display. She started walking to the museum every day, standing by her quilts, telling their stories and the history of Prescott to visitors. Emma was happy at the Pioneer Home for the last three years of her life, now *tied* together again.

One evening her adopted family came to visit. They took her for a ride in her wheelchair. Her adopted grandchildren sat on her lap, dressed her, and fixed her hair. Her adopted son told her he had not been able to care for his own grandparents in their old age, and he wanted to give Emma what he had not been able to give them. She smiled and hugged his whole family. Late that night she died peacefully in her sleep, with a smile on her face. Her adopted son wrapped her in one of her quilts inside her coffin for burial.

It has been said that certain cultures believe each person dies three times. The first time is when the spirit leaves the body, the second is at the funeral, and the third is when people stop talking about the departed. For the next 30 years after I graduated from Prescott College, I pulled out Emma's business card from my wallet from time to time that read, "Emma's Happiness Museum, Remember the Ninety and Nine." I remembered her window display on Valentine's Day with 14 large red hearts made out of cardboard on top of white sand, with a poem written in her large, loopy handwriting on a note card at the center of each heart. I remembered small white plastic doves atop each card and plastic flowers surrounding all. I remembered her being inspired to make a reproduction of Dad Pratt's Good Shepherd quilt (the Ninety and Nine). And wrote this memoir to keep her memory alive for me and others.

In the most basic sense we are just a collection of about 30 to 40 trillion cells, but when those cells are infused with love we are so much more. As human beings we require love to feel healthy, and for many touch is an integral part of love. Amazing as it may sound, each and every one of our cells behaves like a miniature human, says Dr. Bruce Lipton, author of *The Biology of Belief*. Inside you, 40 trillion minute human-like cells work together side-by-side, helping each other accomplish the pumping of your heart, the breathing of your lungs, and all the millions of other tasks that need to happen for the human body to function correctly. When we feel "in love or loved" our cells, which are made of atoms, are actually vibrating from the energy of love! Since change is inevitable and everyone dies, their energy ceases, loved ones embrace that change and manage it by honoring their life at their funeral, and then continue to share their authentic loving memory by stitching them into their collective human memory quilt.

This block of my quilt will be the poem by Arthur Chapman on my favorite quilt of Emma's, which inspired me to write this book, and honors my sense of place, "Out Where the West Begins":

> *Out where the hand clasps a little stronger*
> *Out where the smile dwells a little longer*
> *That's where the west begins.*
> *Out where the sun is a little brighter,*
> *Where the snows that fall are a trifle whiter,*
> *Where the bonds of home are a wee bit tighter*
> *That's where the west begins.*

Nothing could better finish my chronicle in cloth than the blank blocks waiting to be added to my life quilt, when the future becomes the present. I expect that in the end some of my stitching will come out, colors fade, cultural touchstones become irrelevant as my generational quilt blocks unravel, and new blocks are created; but that part of my story will have to be stitched together by my young friends who remember, after my scissors close.

At my celebration of life I want someone to read:

She believed that to find happiness you need love, family, work, spirituality, humor, and especially a sense of place. And that prior planning prevents piss poor performance. Yet change is inevitable, so love it, embrace it, and manage it.

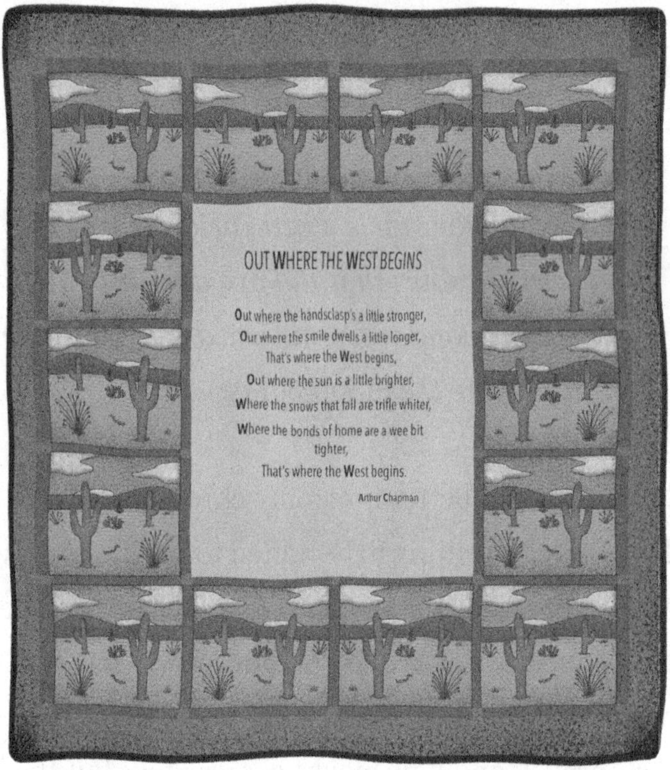

Chapter 29

Stretcher Bars

"Quiltmaking can be a hobby because it gives you enjoyment, but it also comes with a responsibility to artistry ... do it for what you will learn, what you can give to the world, and the fun of it, not to prove something." [41]

Stretcher bars are short slats of wood on a frame that hold several rows of blocks at a time taut while stitching the final quilt together, to ensure even stitches without wrinkles or buckles.

THIRTY-TWO YEARS AFTER IT BEGAN, FOUR CORNERS SCHOOL'S new Canyon Country Discovery Center (CCDC) campus opened its doors for students, educators, young adults, and visitors to make education relevant, meaningful, fun, exciting, and then I retired. By that time, CCDC was providing place-based Science, Technology, Engineering, and Math (STEM) programs for diverse people and communities that built knowledge and health through place-based experiential learning. There was a state-of-the-art campus on 48 acres to serve and inspire visitors, students, educators, families, and researchers with multiple programs based on the natural and human history of the Colorado Plateau. It included a hybrid science and nature facility, informal science center, riparian area, art installations, classroom, night sky observatory, research lab, conference area, nature playscape, cultural learning pavilions, programs, and trails.

During my career, the school transformed lives via a wide range of Colorado Plateau place-based outdoor education programs for over 100,000 participants, ranging in age from six to 90. Under my leadership Four Corners School (FCS) provided several hundred thousand hours of youth and adult service work on public lands, over one million hours of student/youth outdoor education and job training, many hundred thousand hours of adult outdoor education, and almost 200,000 hours of teacher training in place-based outdoor education. The school awarded 200 teacher scholarships for its outdoor classes. Participants repaired or rehabilitated hundreds of miles of roads and trails, restored dozens of springs, and worked to protect more than 42 archaeological sites on public land. The school employed almost 1,000 youth corps crewmembers and leaders in 118 public lands conservation crews. It trained about 1,600 K-8th grade teachers in place-based education in 133 public and Bureau of Indian Affairs (BIA) schools on the Colorado Plateau.

For that work we received 21 local, regional, national, and international awards, including: the 2001 Governor of Utah's Medal for Science and Technology (in science education); the 2001 North American Association for Environmental Education for Outstanding Service to Environmental Education award at the Regional Level; the 2013 Phil James Conservation Award from the Nature Conservancy; and the 2002 Olympics Committee Spirit of the Land Environmental Education Award. This work was all done in one of the most educationally and economically disadvantaged areas of the U.S.

In the future, what CCDC will look like is up to its new leadership. They would be wise to heed scholar Greg Smith, who said in 2016, *"The growing national interest in project-based learning coupled with ... situating these projects in students' home communities can deepen their meaning ... and develop problem-solving skills and the ability to collaborate with others, cultivate a sense of responsibility for the natural environment and the people it supports, instill a recognition of their own capacity to be positive change-makers and leaders ... and be an effective antidote to apathy and alienation ... The environmental and social challenges likely to arise in coming decades will require many people with the kinds of attributes associated with the experience of Place-Based Education."*

Just before I retired, my father and a friend were on my roof replacing and screwing down metal pro-panel sheets. Another friend flew his plane low over my house to check out their work. When he reached his lowest point, my father and friend bent over and dropped their drawers in unison, laughing. After righting themselves and their drawers, my father reached to the sky, both arms overhead and shouted, "I am so proud of you, Janet, and your mother is too!"

I am proud too of how stretcher bars framed my various rows of life quilt blocks to form a responsibility to aging—under fixed conditions—love, family, work, spirituality—and variable conditions—place, humor, the six P's and managing the inevitability of change. And I'm also proud that I was able to integrate how desert plants adapt to inevitably changing life-giving water conditions, into the school's survival strategy, so as to sustain my happiness and the school's positive social change impact.

The stories I've sewn into this memoir describe my journey to craft a place-based life that called me home. They are a love letter to all my family and friends. They describe my faith in the place that helped me find humor and a plan for accepting and managing inevitable change. They are a love letter to everyone that makes a life quilt, from the positive and negative experiences that inevitably change how they live their life, framed and enriched by a "place" that calls them home.

Many nations were framed by a sense of place. The U.S. was founded as a place to escape tyranny, where **all** people are created equal, have equal rights, especially the right to pursue happiness. Israel was founded as a holy place for a Jewish state. The Arab Palestinian state was founded from a strong attachment to the land of their fathers and forefathers. The Navajo Nation was framed by four sacred mountains, which enabled the people to live in harmony with their Creator and nature. In some of these cases, being firmly stuck with an inflexible sense of place has led to anger, hate, violence, war, and endless cycles of poverty; from different interpretations of how to honor and live in that place, demonizing the "other", and being unable to adapt to the inevitable changes in life and the world. Life lived in anger has kept many people locked up in chains, while empathy, love, and a fluid sense of place can set them free.

My key to transforming hate to love was education—education about the fact that the whole world lives on a common living planet, and to survive as a species we must protect and love all life forms equally. Place taught me that under fixed and variable conditions we are all framed by life—that goes by in a blink, a patchwork of colorful, complementary and contrasting, place-based blinks—that when stitched together with intentionality ensures each of us has the opportunity to create our own happiness, feel safe, and work together for the future of our spectacular and unique planet!

As Dr. Martin Luther King, Jr said, "*I have decided to stick with love. Hate is too great a burden to bear.*"

ONE FINAL QUILT BLOCK WILL BE OF AN AIRPLANE FLYING AND TWO BARE BOTTOMS WITH SMILES ON THEM.

Afterword

....

"Some quilts were intended to be works of art rather than ordinary bed covers. And some quiltmakers were more truly artists than ordinary seamstresses ... (and took) quiltmaking beyond the ordinary into the realm of art." [42]

....

To grow an ordinary life into a work of art is to find happiness through finding one's sense of place. Herein are my place-based memories, stuffed in file folders, stored away, worn from repeated examination, and many edits to my perspective. At different times I pull out these dog-eared crumpled scraps of cloth, ponder where I have been, how it still influences me, and what I want to do during the rest of my life.

Over the course of my life every place and person I met produced specific emotions that led me toward a perspective, based on the memories of that place or person. Whether I felt love, compassion, fear, anger, safety, understanding, hurt, or just pure joy, having perspective and empathy helped me know my happy place and happy person(s) that formed within me a commitment to place as a path to love. Place became the center of my life quilt's love story.

From the blocks of elements that permeated my life's happiness—love, family, work, spirituality, sense of place, humor, life planning, adaptability to change—I built a quilt sandwich with a top, back, and filler (or batting that makes the quilt warm). I stitched them together from my place-based perspective, and their relative importance created warmth. Love is what blended my life together, binding truth to understanding context, and accepting change.

From the flat, two-dimensional perspective of a drawing carved or painted on a rock, part petroglyph, part pictograph, I wrote and read this story to Emma so very long ago. She was silent for a few moments, then looked at me hard and said slowly, "I agree, perspective is everything."

Since the time of Buddha, Masaw, God, and the Holy people, I have been watching from a rock wall under an overhang. I don't know who or what Buddha, Masaw, God, or the Holy people are, but I have heard them mentioned by the two-legged creatures. But, I just watch from my rock surface and listen.

A tiny eight-legged, black creature walks across my face, stands still awhile and then from a thread, freefalls to the ground. As it crawls into a crack in the rock, I lose sight of it. But then ... A slightly larger four-legged green creature darts quickly from the same crack. It extends a fleshy part of its face rapidly in and out and woosh, the eight-legged creature is stuck to it and disappears. I think what now and close my eyes?

A much larger two-legged long haired creature walks slowly into my range of view, climbs to me, and sets down a vessel full of red liquid. It puts a small bit of red in its hand and draws a dark red companion for me on the rock. I play my flute louder, my pack grows heavier, and a part between my legs grows larger. I close my eyes, then open them.

Now another two-legged feathered black creature hops into view, struts about with its black webbed fingertips stretched wide. In its mouth it holds a shiny round silver object, which sparkles in the sun, hops to a hole and drops the shiny round object in. With a squawk the creature opens its webbed fingers again, leaps into the air, and lands on the rock above me.

Now, several different two-legged hairy bodied creatures come into my view. They wear orange upper body coverings, longer blue lower body covers, and large round brown head coverings. In one of their hands is a Y-shaped object that sends a small rock through the air. The rock hits the two-legged black feathered creature above me and with a squawk it falls to the ground and does not move again. One of the two-legged says, "Ha, got him. He's real dead, isn't he? Let's kill us some more, they got no real right to live! Let's write our names on the wall here across that picture and carvings, so people know we were really here and have a right to stake our claim."

There it is again, that word "real." I have heard them say that real is something physically experienced by the senses, something that is not an illusion, fantasy, imaginary, or a feeling of intuition. Am I real? Do I have senses? Is the feathered black creature real now that it has no movement? Are those that caused its no movement real? If I cannot leave this rock wall, am I real? I am still watching, listening, and thinking…

Later, I wrote in my journal about what real is to me in three dimensions, from my sense of place on the

Colorado Plateau, where I feel most at home and happy...

Islands of water
Within
A sea of rock.
Remnants of past
Islands atop
Wind streaked spires
Spell out the history
Of exposure.

What new stories must the winds tell if
They could be released
From their commitment
To secrecy!

At first would it be
Of late night prehistoric
Lovemaking or
Coyote pups suckling
Their mother?

Or a mountain lion
Licking the cactus thorns
From between his paw pads-silhouetted
By a backdrop of
Hundreds of

Wind streaked spires
Covered in the
Blood-red glow
Of sunset.

Later it would be of a new world
Shaped and reshaped by natural elements
Over which we have no control, yet no fear
Shaped and reshaped by other chance elements
Some of which we must take actions to control to ensure our survival
All of which we must love, embrace, and manage.

A sense of place is created from contexts, traces, spaces, and experiences. Contexts are the influences that come from a place creating a sense of understanding on what actions you should take in that place. Traces are the items in a particular place that make the specific place recognizable. Spaces are what come together to create the concept of a place. Experiences are what happens in that place that evoke meaningful important life-changing memories.[43] Research shows that when people pass on their love of a place, and share the connection they have with that place, they form a bonded community.

Finding your place can be a solo activity, found in

partnership with others, or two people can independently form a similar sense of place, discover their bond, and powerfully connect. Since we come into the world alone, our memories and emotional roots are ours alone. Our life contexts, traces, spaces, and experiences, at least to start with, are ours. We may later build a shared set of memories and stories with others, and layer it with our past, but our past will always influence us for better or worse—some of which may have left you a little (or a lot) broken. Without a doubt your life quilt's color recipe and design principles are influenced by your early life. If your early life has created in you a healing heart that attracts broken people, heal yourself and others by taking actions to heal your place, which after all is your heart.

A deep sense of place comes from great intimacy with that place, not unlike the deep intimacy one finds in a soul mate, lover, or partner. Every place, like every person, is elevated by the love and respect shown toward them; by the way their special features are discovered; by what you do to honor, protect, and cherish them; and how you build a sense of safety around each other's brokenness. What makes a place or person special to you is the way it buries itself inside your heart, and requires intentionality to grow.

A sense of place and happiness can grow when shared with someone, by loving, embracing, and managing life's inevitable changes. If you have a similar sense of place with another, deeply respect each other's actions to cherish that place, with courage to have grain-of-sand to landscape level conversations about your place, it can create a much stronger bond of love and sense of safety in a way each understands. Yet since change is inevitable, one's sense of place needs to be fluid and multi-layered to allow for growth.

It's easy to say finding your sense of place is a happy way to live, but actually doing it is more difficult! Using values and beliefs to honor my sense of place has been one of the most challenging parts of my life. With changing views being pushed from every side, actual "fake news," and pressure from people with differing ideas, having the strength to hold on to my sense of place with empathy has been a long, hard, but very worthwhile path. A path I have nurtured and maintained over my life, and plan to for the rest of my days.

....

"If you don't know where you are, you don't know who you are."

\- Wendell Berry

....

Acknowledgements

I want to thank Judith Sumner who shared her wise ideas with me on the first draft. Amy Irvine was my detail editor on early drafts and helped me immensely with structure, voice and purpose. Ellen Meloy, Ann Zwinger, Steve Trimble, Terry Tempest Williams, Peter Ross, Reid and Sari Ross, Pamela Moen, Lavinia Norris Exton, Mary Stewart, Toby McLeod, Hildy Armour, Christine Christensen, David Sobel, and Ricky Begaye read other drafts, gave me wise advice, and encouraged me. Beth Green, Sandy Nelson, BJ Boucher, Emma Kemp, Jane Gerhard, and Kate Winter were my more detail-oriented editors toward the end, and I thank them also.

Thank you especially to Craig Childs for his "well-fitted" foreword.

I also want to thank Mark and Jill Tetreau, Laurene Sinema, and Janet Carruth—Emma's adopted family—who took their time to share her with me. I have fond memories of Emma, but I only knew her for a short time and at her happiest moments. I came to know her much better through interviews with these, her adopted family members, as they shared with me the power of their love for her. The Sharlot Hall Museum in Prescott, Arizona provided me with many articles about Emma and her parents. So, I am indebted to them as well.

Words cannot express my gratitude to Kai Standy for her beautiful illustrations. She "visually got" what I was trying to say very quickly and was a joy to work with. Thank you, Kai, for your artistic skill, eye, and voice, and to Bruce Hucko for being my art coach. Thanks too, go to Jonathan Thompson for his belief in my book as Lost Souls Press.

And, finally, I want to thank my family and friends who have always been there for me, especially my mother and father, who will always be my favorite parents. I am also grateful to Emma herself for just being Emma, an exceptional and inspirational quilter, collector of quilt stories, first-timer, and pursuer of happiness.

Notes

[1] Sunset Books, 4
[2] Punset, 1
[3] Fons, et al, 8
[4] Bass, 3, 5
[5] Jenkins, 7
[6] Jenkins, 6
[7] Fons, et al.
[8] Martone, 2012
[9] Bass, 25
[10] Barnes, 4
[11] Jenkins, et al., 103
[12] Fons, et al., 19
[13] Johnson, 71
[14] Jacobson, 1, 2
[15] Ries, 152 and 126
[16] Bass, 3
[17] Jenkins, et al., 77
[18] Bass, 103
[19] Johnson, 63
[20] Jacobson, 17
[21] Fons, et al., 9
[22] Hagood, 104
[23] Logan, 5
[24] Soltow, XIII
[25] Jenkins, 41
[26] Frost and Stevenson, 3
[27] Fans, et al.,50
[28] National Trust, 2017
[29] Fons, et al, 64
[30] Fons, et al, 56
[31] Bering, 2013
[32] Becker, VIII
[33] Jenkins, et al, 103
[34] Bass, 113
[35] Jenkins, 7
[36] Bass, 41
[37] Bass, 9
[38] Bergland, 2012
[39] Veenhoven, R
[40] Jenkins, et al., 45
[41] Fons, et al, 231
[42] Johnson, 103
[43] Bauers, 2

References

Books

Barnes, Christine, 1997, *The Quilters Guide*, That Patchwork Place Inc., Bothell, WA.

Bass, Charlotte Christianson, 1984, *Appliqué Quiltmaking: Contemporary Techniques with an Amish Touch*, Arco Publishing, New York, NY.

Becker, Joyce R., 1996, *Nature's Patterns: Inspirations and Techniques for Quiltmakers*, The Quilt Digest Press, Chicago, IL.

Better Homes and Gardens, 1977, *Patchwork Quilting*, Better Homes and Gardens Books, Meredith Corporation, Des Moines, Iowa.

Editors of Sunset Books, 1975, *Quilting and Patchwork*, Lane Books, Menlo Park, California.

Editors of Sunset Books, 1982, *Quilting, Patchwork, and Appliqué*, Lane Books, Menlo Park, CA.

Florence, Judy, 1987, *Award-Winning Scrap Quilts*, Wallace-Homestead Book Company, Radnor, PA.

Fons, Marrianne and Porter, Liz. 1993, *Quilters Complete Guide*, Oxmoor House, Birmingham, AL.

Frager, Dorothy. 1983, *The Book of Sampler Quilts*, Chilton Book Company, Radnor, Pennsylvania.

Frost, Helen Young and Stevenson, Pam Knight, 1992, *Grand Endeavors: Vintage Arizona Quilts and Their Makers*, Northland Publishing, Flagstaff, AZ.

Gastineau Channel Historical Society, 2003, *Quilts of Alaska*, Juneau, AZ

Gilbert, Daniel, 2005, *Stumbling on Happiness*, Vintage Book, New York, NY

Goleman, Daniel, 2006, *Social Intelligence*, Bantam Dell, New York, NY

Gould, S. J. (2008). *A Biological Homage to Mickey Mouse.* Ecotone 4(1), 333-340. University of North Carolina, Wilmington. Retrieved January 27, 2013, from Project MUSE database.

Graham, John, 1997, *Outdoor Leadership*, The Mountaineers, Seattle, WA.

Hagood, Carol Cook, 1992, *Quilt with the Best*, Oxmoor House, Birmingham, AL.

Hall, June, et.al, 2001, *Quilts of Alaska*, Gastineau Channel Historical Society, Juneau, AK

Jacobson, Anthony and Jeanne, 1993, *Quilting Around Your Home: Decorating with Quilts You Can Make*, Chilton Book Company, Radnor, PA.

Jenkins, Susan and Seward, Linda, 1991, *The American Quilt Story*, Rodale Press, Emmaus, PA.

Johnson, Mary Elizabeth, 1984, *A Garden of Quilts*, Oxmoor House, Birmingham, AL.

Jones, Lila Lee, 2003, *Heartland Quilts*, Chitra Publications, Montrose, PA.

Juster, Norton, 1961, *The Phantom Tollbooth*, Windward Books/Random House, New York, NY.

Kiracofe, Roderick, and Kile, Michael, 1983, *The Quilt Digest*, Kiracofe and Kile Publishing, San Francisco, CA.

Kubzansky, Laura, and Viswanath, K. Vish, *The Science of Happiness: New Discoveries for a More Joyful Life*, Time Inc. Books, 2016

Levitin, Daniel J., 2006. *This Is Your Brain on Music: The Science of a Human Obsession*, Penguin Group, New York, NY

Logan, Diann, 1987, *Designs in Patchwork*, Oxmoor House, Birmingham, AL.

Louv, Richard, 2005, *Last Child in the Woods: Saving our Children from Nature-Deficit Disorder*, Algonquin Books of Chapel Hill, NC

McKendry, Ruth, 1997, *Classic Quilts*, Firefly Books, Willowdale, Ontario, Canada.

Milne, Hollie A., 1988, *Crazy but Pieceable*, That Patchwork Place, Bothell, Washington.

O'Bagy Davis, Carolyn, 1997, *Hopi Quilts: Stitched Traditions from an Ancient Community*, Sanpete Publications Tucson, Arizona.

Punset, Eduardo, 2007, *The Happiness Trip*, Chelsea Green Publishing Company, White River Junction, VT.

Quinn, Daniel, 1992, *Ishmael*, Bantam Books, New York, NY.

Ricard, Matthieu, 2003, *A Guide to Developing Life's Most Important Skill—Happiness*, Little, Brown, and Company, New York, NY

Seligman, Martin E.P., 2002, *Authentic Happiness*, Free Press, New York, NY

Seward, Linda, 1987, *Successful Quilting*, Rodale Press, Emmaus, PA.

Singer, 1990, *Quilting by Machine*, Cy DeCrosse Incorporated, Minnetonka, Minnesota.

Soltow Willow Ann, 1991, *Quilting the World Over*, Chilton Book Company, Rodner, PA.

Stegner, Wallace, 1953, *Beyond the Hundredth Meridian*, University of Nebraska Press, Lincoln, NB.

Strachey, Nino, 2016, *Places That Make Us: Research Report*, National Trust, Swindon, Wiltshire, England

Traina, Frank and Darley-Hill, Susan, 1997, *Perspectives in Bioregional Education*, North American Association for Environmental Education, Washington DC.

Turner, Jack, 1996, *The Abstract Wild*, The University of Arizona Press, Tucson, AZ.

Zimmer, Marc, 2005, *Glowing Genes: A Revolution in Biotechnology*, Prometheus Books, Amherst, NY, pages 40-45.

News Articles

The Prescott Courier, Obituaries, page 2C May 1, 1988,

Westward, "Emma's Happiness Museum," March 10, 1978, Claudette Simpson

The Prescott Courier, "One Picture's Worth 1,000 Words," October 15, 1982, Claudette Simpson

QNM, "Arizona Quilter of the Year: Emma Andres," April 1984, Carruth, Janet & Sinema, Laurene

Sharlot Hall Museum, "Emma Andres (b. 1902-d. 1988)," March 26, 2015, Dr. Sue Kessel

The Prescott Daily Courier, "Emma's Happiness Museum," April, 1984 Lorine Morris

The Prescott Daily Courier, "Prescott Quilter Emma Andres Was One of Nation's honored," May, 1994, Mary Lin

Arizona Days and Ways Magazine, "A Collector of Friendships," December 1, 1957, Hermine Megargee

Quilters Journal, "Emma Andres Quilts and Her Happiness Museum," Summer 1981, Joyce Gross

The Prescott Courier, "Café Location Once Housed Quaint, Unique Museum," August 5, 1999, John Schwartz

Journal Articles

Ault, C. R. (2008). "Achieving querencia: Integrating a Sense of Place with Disciplined Thinking." *Curriculum Inquiry*, 38, 605-637.

Carruth, Janet and Sinema, Laurene, "Emma M. Andres and Her Six Grand Old Characters," *Uncoverings*, 1990, The Group, Mill Valley, CA.

Cowley, Geoffery, "The Science of Happiness," *Newsweek*, September 16, 2002.

Ries, Rebecca, A., "Stitched in Place, Stitches in Time: Relationships of Quilts, Quiltmaking, and Landscape," *Uncoverings*, 1996, The Group, Mill Valley, CA.

Slater, Lauren, "C'mon Get Happy," *Rosie Magazine*, 8/2002.

The Happiness Research Institute, "The Happy Danes: Exploring the Reasons Behind the High Levels of Happiness in Denmark," 2014

Website Links and Articles

Anderberg, Jeremy, "The Art of Topophilia: 7 Ways to Love the Place You Live," https://www.artofmanliness.com/character/advice/ the-art-of-topophilia-7-ways-to-love-the-place-you-live/, October 1, 2019

Bauers, Kelsey, "Perspective of Place," https://maptia.com/kbauers/stories/perspective-of-place

Bergland, Christopher, 2012, "The Neurochemicals of Happiness," *Psychology Today*, blog post https://www.psychologytoday.com/blog/the-athletes-way/201211/the-neurochemicals-happiness

Bering, Jesse, Ian Stevenson, "Case for the Afterlife: Are We 'Skeptics' Really Just Cynics?" https://blogs.scientificamerican.com/bering-in-mind/ian-stevensone28099s-case-for-the-afterlife-are-we-e28098skepticse28099-really-just-cynics/

Brown, Patricia Leigh, "Gone but Never Forgotten in a Quilt," December 16, 2020. *New York Times* https://www.nytimes.com/2020/12/16/arts/design/quilt-art-women-injustice.html

Gross, Joyce, Emma Andres, "The Quilt Index," *Quilter's Journal*, Summer 1981 http://www.quiltindex.org/journals/article.php?Akid=2-B-45

Hamer, Dean, "The God Gene: How Faith Is Hardwired Into Our Genes," https://www.nature.com/articles/ ng1204-1241, Doubleday 2004

Helliwell, John; Layard, Richard; and Sachs, Jeffrey, and Jan Emmanuel De Neve, Co-Editors; Lara Aknin, Haifang Huang and Shun Wang, Associate Editors; and Sharon Paculor, Production Editor, "World Happiness Report, 2020," https://worldhappiness.report/ed/2020/#read

Lambert, Craig, "The Science of Happiness," January-February 2007, *Harvard Magazine*, http://harvardmagazine.com/2007/01/the-science-of-happiness.html

Manning-Schaffel, Vivian, "Why Some Songs Make Us Cry," NBC News, July 21, 2017, https://www.nbcnews.com/better/health/why-do-certain-songs-make-us-cry-ncna784801

Martone, Robert, "Scientists Discover Children's Cells Living in Mothers' Brains," *Scientific American*, December 4, 2012 http://www.scientificamerican.com/article/scientists-discover-childrens-cells-living-in-mothers-brain/

Nabhan, Gary Pail, "The Wild, the Domesticated, and the Coyote-Tainted: The Trickster and the Tricked in Hunter-Gatherer Versus Farmer Folklore," https://garynabhan.com/fileman/dl/pdf/Amadeo-Chapter-7.pdf

Rimer, Sara, "The Biology of Emotion: And What It May Teach Us About Helping People to Live Longer," *Health and Happiness*, Winter 2011, Harvard School of Public Health. http://www.hsph.harvard.edu/ news/magazine/happiness-stress-heart-disease/

Scheer, Roddy, "Can Waterfalls Make You Happy?," *Health News Digest*, June 3, 2015.

St Louis Post Dispatch, June 8, 1980, https://www.newspapers.com/newspage/139629580

Tierney, John, "What's so Funny? Well, Maybe Nothing," March 13, 2007, *New York Times*, www.nytimes.com/2007/03/13/science/13tier.html?ex=1 175400000&en=0aef64611b713564&ei=5070

United Press International, "Pennies From Heaven For Firefly Catchers," August 24, 1987 http://articles.chicagotribune.com/1987-08-24/business/8703040337_1_fireflies-sclerosis-and-heart-disease-shark-tank

Veenhoven, R., "World Database of Happiness," Erasmus University Rotterdam, The Netherlands, http://worlddatabaseofhappiness.eur.nl.

Yasmin Anwar, "Bach to the Blues: Our Emotions Match Music to Colors," UC Berkeley News Center, May 16, 2013.

Personal Interviews

Mark Treteau, March 1997.

Lorene Sinema and Janet Caruth, March 1997.

Biographies

Janet Ross – Author

With a B.A. in Outdoor Education and an M.S. in Experiential Education, Janet started the non-profit Four Corners School of Outdoor Education in 1984 – based on her love for the Colorado Plateau, desire to teach others about the need to understand and protect it, and belief in the power of place-based education to change lives. Prior to founding Four Corners School, she worked for over 15 years as a backcountry ranger and wilderness specialist for the National Park Service, Bureau of Land Management, and U.S. Forest Service, and as an educator and guide for the National Outdoor Leadership School, Colorado Outward Bound, Prescott College, and other outdoor programs. She retired at the end of 2016 after completing the construction of the Canyon Country Discovery Center, a portal to place-based education about the Colorado Plateau and new campus for Four Corners School on 48 acres north of Monticello, Utah.

Janet published numerous articles in professional journals over 32 years as Executive Director of Four Corners School of Outdoor Education. Over those years the School earned 21 local, regional, and national awards for its place-based education programs, including the 2002 Olympics Committee Spirit of the Land Award, 2001 Governor of Utah's Medal for Science and Technology (in science education), 2001 North American Association for Environmental Education for Outstanding Service to Environmental Education at the Regional Level, and 2005 Utah Society for Environmental Education's Program and Educator of the Year. The Discovery and Learning Channels, CBS, NBC, and various newspapers have written about her work as a pioneer in outdoor, place-based, and environmental education.

Kai Standy – Illustrator

Kai Standy (Kylee Manuelito) is a Navajo artist and animator from the Navajo Nation. She is from the Ta'neeszahnii (Tangled Clan), Tábąąhá (Water's Edge Clan), Mą'ii deeshgiizhinii (Coyote Pass Clan), and Tó'aheedlíinii (Flowing Water Clan).

She works to expand the art of Animation into Indigenous communities by creating original works and bringing stories to life, one frame at a time. She has been drawing and animating for 7 years and working to create her own visual story and animated short film. To see more of her work, go to: https://linktr.ee/standy1321.

Made in the USA
Las Vegas, NV
16 September 2023

77664420R00174